AMERICAN DEMOCRACY
AND
SECONDARY EDUCATION

A Study of Some Tendencies and Conceptions
of Youth Education in the United States

By KENNETH D. NORBERG, Ph.D.

TEACHERS COLLEGE, COLUMBIA UNIVERSITY
CONTRIBUTIONS TO EDUCATION, NO. 886

Published with the Approval of
Professor John L. Childs, Sponsor

Bureau of Publications
TEACHERS COLLEGE, COLUMBIA UNIVERSITY,
NEW YORK, 1943

COPYRIGHT, 1944, BY KENNETH D. NORBERG

PRINTED AND BOUND IN THE U. S. A. BY
KINGSPORT PRESS, INC., KINGSPORT, TENN.

ACKNOWLEDGMENT

THE writer is grateful to the many persons who aided him in the completion of this study. In particular, special thanks are due Professor John L. Childs, the sponsor, for exacting criticism, for wise guidance, and for constant encouragement throughout the course of the work.

Grateful acknowledgment is made to Professor L. Thomas Hopkins, to Professor Hollis L. Caswell, and to Professor William B. Featherstone for stimulation in the initial formulation of the problem, and for many helpful suggestions in the writing. Also, the writer is deeply indebted to Dawson Hales for reading and commenting on the manuscript in its various stages, and to Adalyn Norberg, who gave constant help in its preparation.

K. D. N.

CONTENTS

AMERICAN DEMOCRACY
AND
SECONDARY EDUCATION

INTRODUCTION

PROBABLY most American educators who have considered the evolution of the secondary school in the United States would now agree that it has reached a period of critical transition. The American tradition of equality of educational opportunity grew out of conditions which also supported the rise of a unitary public school system offering free education for all. The extension of the common school to include the secondary level was a unique development in the history of education. As such, the secondary school was addressed to the common needs of American youth and carried with it the promise of democratic equality of opportunity which was also guaranteed by the abundance of a great industrial system based upon plentiful resources. Never completely realized, the universal public high school was impeded in its development and performance by changing conditions and dislocations for which our social and economic life had developed no adequate plan nor effective measure. This study therefore considers the problem of youth education as defined by the partial failure of its democratic promise, and also by social and economic conditions which have obstructed the fulfillment of the role of the democratic school. The problems of secondary education are viewed as continuous with the problems of American industrial democracy.

In a primary sense this study is an attempt to appraise the secondary school from the standpoint of the integral relationship between the "youth problem" and the problem of youth education. Its purpose, in this regard, is to examine critically certain tendencies and conceptions of secondary education with reference to the democratic tradition of the unitary public school as it took form in American life. It should be understood that the writer's intention is not to give an encyclopedic account of the various factors which influenced the development of the American secondary school, nor to attempt to predict its future course. The historical aspect of the study is limited to the discussion of pertinent factors which contributed to the development of the democratic conception of youth education in this country, and to its somewhat ambiguous and confused status at the present moment.

The American high school has long been charged with the failure to develop an instructional program adequately suited to the needs of the large majority of its students. The "college-preparatory" curriculum has been widely discredited as an aristocratic program representing an outmoded tradition, or as catering to a minority group, while the proponents of the "new" curriculum have joined in mounting criticism of the "formal," the "classical," and the "traditional." An increasing number of American educators are apparently prepared to accept a secondary school program based on the needs and interests, or functionally developmental activities, of youth. But it is not clear that many educators are prepared to accept the urgent implications of such a program, particularly with regard to the problems which in times of peace have been represented by the attentuated and often isolated status of vocational education, by youth unemployment and the symptomatic youth work agencies.

If our secondary schools are now undergoing a critical transition the writer's purpose is to consider those factors in the total complex of developments which bear most directly upon his problem. From the standpoint of competing educational theories and movements a good deal of the discussion turns upon Progressivism in secondary education for the primary reason that Progressive education probably represents the present outstanding force in the reconstruction of the traditional school. The second and equally important reason is that certain root conceptions in Progressive education seem to provide the basis of a democratic philosophy of education, whereas Progressive theory and practice have somewhat persistently failed to face the full social and educational implications of such a position. In this sense, Progressive education is considered as a movement which offers educational alternatives to the traditional school program but has not adequately accepted the obligation to deal with refractory and integrally related social factors in the problem.

The Progressive conception of a secondary school based on functional activities of youth is examined with reference to the thesis that such a program depends upon conditions which are not merely pedagogical and methodological, but something more. It is with respect primarily to the possible limitations of such a "methodological" and "pediatrical" Progressivism that two opposing positions are considered. But these positions are also examined as representing broader tendencies and conceptions which are not wholly confined to Progressive education.

In opposition to Progressive conceptions of secondary education, the case for the "subject" curriculum is reviewed in the representative materials of a prominent educator who has long argued for the values of sustained and systematic learning based upon proper recognition of the demands of the intrinsic relations of the object, on the one hand, and the proper exercise of distinctively "human" capacities, on the other. His position is not viewed merely as a defense of the traditional school, but it does provide a basis for the appraisal of certain educational practices (whether traditional or not) which help to re-evaluate, or to gain a better perspective of Progressive and other tendencies related to the problem of the study. In this wise the writer's purpose is to explore the meaning and function of "organized" subject matter in the school program and to define its relation to the "activity" curriculum. Among others, the conclusion is reached that to insure continuity of group behavior, the meaning of subject matter in the high school curriculum must be related to the progressive stages by which the immature individual is gradually inducted into more and more inclusive social activities which involve a relatively high degree of organization and the increasing use of symbols and relatively fixed meanings. Here, as throughout the study, the emphasis is not on the content of the curriculum, as such, but on its changing function with respect to the induction of the maturing individual into the life of the social group.

In reviewing the "intellectualistic" argument against the

"new" education the problem is further refined with respect to the criticism that Progressive education is forever lost in a "positivistic" morass of experimental and tentative conclusions in which certainties are prohibited, and clearly defined aims impossible. The implications of the intellectualistic approach to secondary education are discussed with particular reference to the problems of educational planning in a democracy, and to the possible limitations of a curriculum based merely upon the "expressed needs" of pupils as formulated by local planning groups. The contra-experimentalistic implications of "intellectualism" are examined and totally rejected, but the positive purpose of the study at this point is to give recognition to the importance of the *structure* of human behavior in educational planning, and to raise the question whether the Progressive secondary school has suffered from the lack of aims which were sufficiently inclusive and well-defined to incorporate the actual social and economic conditions of its educational ideals.

Such criticisms of Progressive education carry enough truth to be suggestive, if not challenging. However, the final problem, so far as this study is concerned, is not primarily whether the Progressive secondary school is based on an adequate philosophy of education. It is rather to interpret certain fundamental difficulties of the secondary school as a democratic institution designing to offer essentially equal opportunities for the common personal development and growth of American youth in this industrial society. The conclusions of the study form an appraisal of tendencies and conceptions of secondary education which appear to be central to this problem. They are based on the thesis that a democratic public high school program literally must provide for the gradual and functional absorption of the developing energies of youth into responsible participation in the work and total affairs of the community life.

CHAPTER I

BACKGROUNDS OF THE PROBLEM

In this study American secondary education is considered as an outgrowth of the common school movement. The backgrounds of the early schools in this country were European, but the development of the free public high school in the nineteenth and twentieth centuries was in its main respects peculiarly American.

The Rise of the Common School

From its early beginnings in the vernacular schools of the medieval towns of Europe the rise of the common school [1] was attended by conditions which marked the dissolution of feudal society and the development of the modern industrial liberal-democratic state. Vernacular schools had appeared in the towns of the Netherlands as early as the thirteenth century.[2] By the sixteenth and seventeenth centuries these town schools had reached a state of remarkable development which is generally attributed to economic and political factors involved in the growth of the towns, and especially to the commercial developments of the period in which they emerged. Eby and Arrowood, for instance, cite three factors in the growth of the town schools: commercialism, democratic government (within the separate towns), and the Reformation.[3]

The origin of the common school has sometimes been attributed to the Reformation, and to Luther, in particular, who was an advocate of free, universal education. Historians do not agree on this point. There has been a tendency in recent years

[1] The modern common school is distinguished from the elementary Latin school which developed in the ancient period. See Edward H. Reisner, *The Evolution of the Common School*, pp. 1 ff. The Macmillan Company, New York, 1930.

[2] Frederick Eby and Charles Flinn Arrowood, *The Development of Modern Education*, p. 61. Prentice-Hall, Inc., New York, 1934.

[3] *Ibid.*, p. 132.

5

to qualify the degree of importance that some placed on the Reformation as a factor in the development of popular education.[4] But whether or not the Reformation was a primary factor in the rise of the common school it appears to have been an important aspect of a complex of social developments which attended the final disintegration of medieval feudalism and the domination of Europe by the Roman Catholic Church. Hayes remarks on the strong rise of national sovereignty in the sixteenth century and the struggle to "bring religion under national control." [5] Nationalists wanted the power and influence of the Church, and at the same time they regarded the established religious hierarchy as a great obstacle to their political aims. The rising capitalists also had an interest in the conflict, which was economic as well as political and religious.[6] Thus, the Reformation may be considered one phase of the rise of the modern, industrial-national state, and as such it was aligned with the social and intellectual developments which gave birth to the common school.

There were, of course, other and more direct educational effects of the Reformation, particularly in the emphasis upon private reading of the Scriptures, the promotion of a legal basis for elementary education in Lutheran Germany, and the important influences of Calvinism and Puritanism in the Dutch and English colonial schools.[7] But the peculiarly religious character of these developments should not obscure other equally fundamental factors in the rise of the common school.

The invention and development of power-driven machines and the corporate form of industrial enterprise, the growth of the cities, the rise of political democracy, and the beginnings of nationalism: these, in the main, were the foundations of universal public education. Following the rise of secular authority in the sixteenth century, the national state emerged as the domi-

---

[4] Edward H. Reisner, *The Evolution of the Common School*, pp. 21 ff. The Macmillan Company, New York, 1930. Also Eby and Arrowood, *op. cit.*, esp. pp. 82–100.

[5] Carlton J. H. Hayes, *A Political and Cultural History of Modern Europe*, Vol. 1, p. 149. The Macmillan Company, New York, 1933.

[6] *Ibid.*, p. 150.

[7] Reisner, *op. cit.*, Chap. III.

nant form of political organization in the seventeenth and eighteenth centuries. The French Revolution brought a common national consciousness to the masses of the French people, and with it, plans for the educational inculcation of the revolutionary ideals in the interests of national solidarity. Reisner points out how Napoleon's defeat of Prussia helped to precipitate the rise of German nationalism, which was in turn the basis of a national system of compulsory education under secular control.[8] In the meantime important technical developments were preparing the way for modern industry, the growth of cities, and the rise of corporate industrial organization and wage labor, all of which were to have important effects upon the common school. The beginnings of political democracy were obviously of great significance but their educational effects appeared with the later and somewhat gradual extension of political liberties.

Along with the predisposing social and political conditions of the sixteenth, seventeenth, and eighteenth centuries the intellectual foundations of the common school were laid in the scientific world-view and the philosophy of liberalism. The elevation of human reason and the humanitarian aspects of the "enlightenment" were a fertile ground for the promotion of schemes of popular education.[9] Bacon had stressed the rise of the scientific method to improve human welfare. Comenius, Pestalozzi, and others helped to develop the educational implications of the scientific movement and to show the importance of shared intelligence as a basis for the development of a new technical and industrial world. Great influence has been attributed to Pestalozzi, especially.[10] Cordorcet, Jefferson, and others were also sensitive to the political implications of the common school. They shared the democratic ideal that every man should have in education the opportunity to make an intelligent contribution to the social enterprise and to share in its benefits.

But the ideals of the liberals and educational reformers were

---

[8] Reisner, *op. cit.*, pp. 214 ff.
[9] Hayes, *op. cit.*, pp. 551 ff.
[10] Reisner, *op. cit.*, Chap. XI. Also Eby and Arrowood, *op. cit.*, Chap. XVII.

not to be realized at once. In the nineteenth century the development of universal elementary education was a slow process, and it was not until the seventies and eighties that laws were passed in England and France to provide for compulsory and universal attendance in the elementary schools.[11] It is interesting that manhood suffrage in France and the wide extension of suffrage in England belonged, roughly, to the period when the elementary schools were being universalized, and that the extension of the right to vote was accompanied by the demand for universal, compulsory education.[12]

The close connection between the industrial revolution, the massing of workers in the cities, and the rising political influence of the working groups need not be recounted here. Whether the extension of suffrage be considered the result of the struggles of a self-conscious working class which sought to improve its lot and to gain a more satisfactory share in the benefits of the industrial enterprise, or whether it be considered in some other light, there can be little question that the development of political democracy in the nineteenth century had an economic base and that the expansion of the common school was largely conditioned by underlying industrial and political changes.[13] The intimate relationship between the rise of the common school and its social foundations becomes even more strikingly apparent if one compares the American development with that which occurred in Europe.

Disregarding, for the moment, more recent changes in the educational systems of Europe, the common school of the early nineteenth century in Europe obviously was a school for the children of the masses as opposed to those of the privileged classes. The opportunities for free education were restricted. Such schools as were provided through "charity" or public support for the children of the poor were not affected by equalitarian conceptions. It is probably safe to say that the function of the common school at that time was primarily to promote

[11] Reisner, op. cit., pp. 247, 268.
[12] Ibid., p. 267.
[13] Ibid., Chap. XIII, XXVI.

literacy, to teach the rudiments of religious faith, and to incul-
cate the nationalistic ideals. In Prussia, where the development
of tax-supported elementary education was early promoted for
nationalistic purposes, the case was not essentially different.
Here, as in England and France, the conception of a more liberal type of elementary education was present. The economic
and political foundations of a truly liberal common school were
not present, however. And thus, a Prussian Minister of Education was led to make the following significant comment, the
concluding point in a statement of educational aims:

> . . . I regard popular education as truly more than a scanty in-
> struction in the bare instrumentalities of culture—reading, writing,
> and arithmetic. On the other hand, I do not think that the prin-
> ciples enunciated will raise the common people out of the sphere
> designated for them by God and human society. I think rather that
> they are able to make the common man's lot agreeable and profitable
> to him.[14]

Although the case has been somewhat altered in recent years
it must be remembered that the European secondary schools of
the nineteenth century were discontinuous with the common
schools. The upper schools provided a liberal education (which
was also occupational in character) for pupils of rank, and to
some extent for those of special ability. Such training led to
positions of political leadership or to the professions. The common schools remained the "closed-in" [15] schools of the children
of the working classes and no way was provided for them to
advance to a higher stage of education which might lead to a
change in social status.

Beginnings of the American Public Schools

In the colonial period and early post-Revolutionary times the
American schools followed the same general pattern of the dual
educational system in Europe. In the colonies there were two
educational systems, one serving (as Curti puts it) the "mer-
chants, planters, clergy, and lawyers"—the other serving the

[14] Quoted by Reisner, *op. cit.*, p. 234.
[15] Reisner, *op. cit.*, pp. 551–552.

"common people."[16] The tax-supported town schools of New England were democratic in principle and their widely recognized value as setting a precedent for free education in this country should not be discounted. But even the early town schools were part of a general pattern of class education.[17] The Latin grammar schools were privately supported, fee schools, as were the academies which arose near the end of the colonial period. As in Europe, the function of the secondary school was to provide a college preparatory training for the sons of wealthier families who were planning to enter positions of leadership in the church, the law, or in business life. Moreover, the schools which provided this type of training were discontinuous with the common schools.[18]

The rise and decline of the privately maintained academies reflected the transition in American education to a new type of secondary school. The academies flourished in the years following the Revolution and especially in the early part of the nineteenth century. They marked the decline of the dual educational system in the United States but they were also peculiarly American in the range and "practical" character of their interests.[19] To some extent they entered into competition with the colleges. The approach of a new phase of secondary education was suggested by the fact that some academies offered a kind of terminal education, and were sometimes known as the "people's colleges." Briggs remarks that,

> In the earlier days the academies were "bound up with the interests of the common people," planned to provide for their assured needs and to create new intellectual wants, not primarily preparing students for college, and in some cases training teachers. . . .[20]

The first public high school was established in Boston in 1821,

---

[16] Merle Curti, *The Social Ideas of American Educators*, Report of the Commission on the Social Studies, Pt. X, p. 21. Charles Scribner's Sons, New York, 1935.

[17] *Ibid.*, pp. 21 ff.

[18] Reisner, *op. cit.*, p. 362.

[19] I. L. Kandel, *History of Secondary Education*, pp. 397–401. Houghton Mifflin Company, Boston, 1930.

[20] Thomas H. Briggs, *Secondary Education*, p. 80. The Macmillan Company, New York, 1935.

and after that time the number of tax-supported secondary schools gradually increased. By 1874 the principle of the tax-supported secondary school was well established. The decision of the well-known Kalamazoo case in that year was based on the main issue of *whether the common schools of the state included the high schools.* The decision in favor of tax-supported second-ary education has generally been taken as a major incident in the development of the free public high school.[21] By 1872, two years before the Kalamazoo decision, the number of public high schools in the United States was about 500.[22] Stout's estimate of 100 high schools for the year 1860 [23] gives some indication of the rapid growth of the secondary school following that time, but by 1890 the number of high schools reporting to the United States Commissioner of Education had risen to 2,526. The re-markable development of the universal secondary school was under way.

Many historians have pointed out that the emergence of the free public high school as a part of the common school system in the United States was unique. Reisner attributes this pecu-liar development to "economic and social circumstances which had their rise in the great endowment of cheap land." [24] There are probably few who would not agree that at least the great resources and rapidly increasing wealth of the American nation in the latter part of the nineteenth century had simplified the fiscal problem of public education. Jefferson and other leaders of the early years of the Republic had entertained inspiring con-ceptions of the role of public schools in the life of the new na-tion, but as Beard points out,

    . . . the times were not propitious for bringing them to fruition. The great social and economic forces which were to call them into being some forty or fifty years after the adoption of the Constitu-tion had not yet appeared. The population of America consisted of

[21] Kandel, *op. cit.,* pp. 444 ff.
[22] Calvin Olin Davis, *Our Evolving High School Curriculum,* p. 31. World Book Company, New York, 1927.
[23] John Elbert Stout, *The Development of High-School Curricula in the North Central States from 1860 to 1918,* p. 16. The University of Chicago Press, Chi-cago, 1921.
[24] Reisner, *op. cit.,* p. 363.

between three and four million persons, thinly scattered over a wide area. Rural civilization predominated. As late as 1820 less than five per cent of the total population lived in the thirteen cities of 8000 or over.[25]

The tremendous changes that occurred in American life before the close of the nineteenth century: the industrial development, the growth and urbanization of the population, the development of the railroads and the beginnings of a national system of communication—all of these were obviously part of a great revolution which made the unitary public school possible.

The economic and social conditions in the United States which attended the early rise of the public secondary school were also unique. The conditions for social mobility: the democratic tradition, the "leveling" effects of frontier life, and the rich opportunities for personal advancement through the application of newly developed technical instruments to a great virgin continent, were without parallel in the history of the world. These factors, undoubtedly, were highly important in the establishment of a system of "classless" education. An expanding industrialism combined with seemingly endless resources had provided the ideal foundation for the development of political democracy, and with it, the rise of the common school.

As significant, perhaps, as the great natural and industrial resources of the expanding national economy was an almost boundless faith in the possibilities of democracy and free land. Beard points out that as late as 1852 debaters in Congress were arguing that it would take from 400 to 900 years to dispose of the remaining public lands, considering the amount in the hands of the government and the rate of sale at that time.[26] He adds that ". . . With such a pleasing economic prospect spread out before them, the sponsors of public education could with good reason proclaim opportunity; committed to the principle

---

[25] Educational Policies Commission, *The Unique Function of Education in American Democracy*, p. 27. National Education Association of the United States and the Department of Superintendence, Washington, D. C., 1937.

[26] *Ibid.*, p. 47.

of equality for all, they could plead for equal educational facilities." [27]

The rise of equalitarian democracy and the strong individualistic temper of the middle and later years of the nineteenth century were of the essence of the period in which the unitary public school system took form. Equality of opportunity was one of the dominant ideas of those years, and it was this conception that lay at the root of a system of popular education that would provide an equal start in life to all American citizens. "Education was regarded as an aid in assuring equality of preparation for economic opportunity." [28] Political democracy, however, was also an independent force in the development of the common school system. On the one hand it was a tool in the hands of the enfranchised groups, such as Labor, which was strongly interested in the public school movement, and on the other, it was used as an argument for universal education on the grounds that an unenlightened electorate would be a dangerous threat to democracy itself.[29]

Foundations of Universal Secondary Education

Despite the economic and political conditions which gave rise to a unitary public school system in the United States, the secondary school of the late nineteenth century was still selective in the character of its attendance. The continuous educational ladder was open to all, but the secondary school was yet to become the educational institution for the masses of American youth. However, important social changes were already expanding the function of the common school. Changes in the population, in the family, in the character of employment and economic opportunity, were creating tremendous new responsibilities for the public school, and for secondary education in particular. To cite only the most pertinent factors—

The increasing mechanization of agriculture, the one-crop farm, and the resulting displacement of rural labor combined with the tendency of industrialism to create an ever-growing

[27] *Ibid.*, p. 47.
[28] *Ibid.*, p. 46.
[29] Reisner, *op. cit.*, pp. 325–326.

urban population was one factor. As late as 1840 about 90 per cent of the population was rural, as compared with only about 45 per cent in 1930.[30] In the meantime, the end of the geographic frontier, the technical displacement of labor, and the aging of the total population [31] were gradually contracting employment possibilities under a wage-labor system. All of these changes were multiplied in effect by important economic factors (especially after 1930) with results which affected great masses of American youth.

The American family was also undergoing almost revolutionary changes during the rise of the unitary public school. As compared with the relatively large, stable, and self-contained economic unit of the early agrarian family, the modern industrial and highly urbanized population had produced a family pattern which was smaller, less stable, and much less of an economic unit. The average size of the American household group in 1850 was 5.6 persons as compared with 4.1 in 1930.[32] In 1870 the ratio of divorces to marriages was one to thirty-three; in 1930, one to less than six.[33] The decline of the family as a producing economic unit requires little documentation. The early agrarian family which provided for most of its needs is in telling contrast to the family group of the modern city in which many of the domestic functions, such as food preparation, clothes making, and laundering, have been shifted in whole or in part to outside agencies. The rising number of married and gainfully employed women, alone, is a significant index of the declining importance of the family as an economic unit.[34]

Closely associated with these changes was the diminishing

[30] Leslie A. Gould, *American Youth Today*, p. 232. Random House, New York, 1940.

[31] In 1850 the ratio of adults (over 20) to youth (under 16) was about 9 to 10. By 1938 it had changed to about 21 to 10. (From figures cited by Homer P. Rainey, *How Fare American Youth?*, pp. 41–42. D. Appleton-Century Company, New York, 1938.)

[32] Lloyd Allen Cook, *Community Backgrounds of Education*, p. 126. McGraw-Hill Book Company, New York, 1938.

[33] *Ibid.*, p. 127.

[34] *Ibid.*, p. 127. (The number of working married women increased 60 per cent between 1920 and 1930 while the number of married women in the total population increased only 23 per cent.)

function of the family as an educational unit. Family education was largely deprived of its occupational setting.[35] The domestic and recreational functions of the family were dispersed, and many forces conspired against its integrity as a social unit.

The changing industrial and social conditions which have been cited combined with obvious effects to prolong the period of dependency of American youth, and to shift an increasing measure of educational responsibility to public agencies, and especially to the public secondary school. In the meantime the vast productive machinery of the nation continued to expand and to support a mounting national income which made possible the growth of universal secondary education.

The Changing Function of the Secondary School

The fivefold increase in the number of public high schools between 1870 and 1890 has already been cited. In 1890 the number of students enrolled in the public high schools was 202,963.[36] By 1910 the total enrollment figure had reached 915,061. This was doubled by 1920 and more than doubled again in the next ten years, reaching a total of 4,145,669 by 1930.[37] Between 1900 and 1938 the high school enrollment had increased almost 1200 per cent, whereas the number of persons 14 to 17 years of age in the total population had increased about 60 per cent.[38] Thus, it is a safe estimate that the secondary school grew about 20 times faster than the youth population. From a relatively small and highly selected population the secondary school enrollment has changed to one which is widely inclusive in its range of abilities and interests, as well as the range of its social and economic backgrounds.

The story of the changing high school curriculum has been

[35] The important educational implications of this development were pointed out by John Dewey in *School and Society*, pp. 6 ff. The University of Chicago Press, Chicago, 1900.
[36] Federal Security Agency, United States Office of Education, Bulletin 1940, No. 2, *Statistics of Public High Schools*, Chap. V, pp. 20–21.
[37] *Ibid.*, pp. 20–21.
[38] United States Department of Commerce, Bureau of the Census, *Statistical Abstract of the United States*, 1940, p. 113.

told many times. An exhaustive account of the changes in the American culture which affected the development of the program of the public school is not required for the purposes of this study. It is merely noted that the effects, in education, of the development of modern science and technology, alone, can hardly be overestimated. Many observers have recorded the educational demands of modern industry and commerce with their increasing diversification of occupational function and knowledge. Other factors, such as the rise of an indigenous American art, no doubt also played important roles in the development of the modern high school program. However, the broad and rather obvious effects of such influences are not immediately pertinent to the problem of this study.

On the other hand, some indication of specific changes and trends in the high school program should be noted. Of particular interest are such matters as the sheer expansion of the curriculum, the influence of uncoordinated social pressures in determining changes, and the growing interest in vocational education.

From this point on, the discussion of this chapter is primarily concerned with tensions that have developed in an educational system in which the traditional opposition of "academic" and "vocational" education has become one of the most significant corollaries of a "youth problem" which is educational and broadly social at the same time.

The practice of offering two high school courses, one to prepare for "life" and the other for college, had become fairly common before 1860. In fact, the twofold function of the public secondary school can be traced back to the very beginnings of the high school movement.[39] Differentiation, however, was not limited to the two broad functions of college and "life" preparation, even in the middle years of the nineteenth century. In the period from 1860 to 1865 Stout reports that 12 of 20 representative high schools offered a single course, whereas six of the schools offered two, and the remaining two schools offered

[39] John Elbert Stout, *The Development of High School Curricula in the North Central States from 1860 to 1918*, p. 5. The University of Chicago Press, Chicago, 1921.

three courses each. By 1896 the number of schools offering a single course had changed to 25 out of a group of 60, while the total number of courses offered had increased to seven in the case of one school. In 1860–1865, the average number of courses in schools offering more than one curriculum was 2.25. This figure had increased to about 3.17 by the close of the century, and 36 titles were used to designate the various courses offered. During the intervening period the proportion of schools offering single courses had decreased from 60 per cent to approximately 42 per cent.[40]

After 1900 the expansion of the high school curriculum continued at an accelerating pace. In a study of 60 secondary schools for the years 1906–1911, Stout found 46 different titles of curricula with the number of parallel courses per school running as high as six.[41] In the period 1915–1918 the number of titles of courses had increased to 88 and one school was offering 19 separate curricula.[42]

In 1890 the Annual Report of the Commissioner of Education listed registrations in the public high schools under nine subject headings—these representing the scope of the secondary curriculum at that time.[43] By 1915 the number of subject offerings in the high schools had increased to 26.[44] This number is low, partly because of the fact that subjects not generally offered in most of the states were not included in the Office of Education reports prior to 1922. In any event, the number of subject offerings reported in 1915 had more than doubled by 1922, and more than doubled again by 1928, finally reaching a total of 206 in 1934.[45] Homer P. Rainey cites a similar development in college and university education:

[40] *Ibid.*, p. 52. (It should be added that Stout found it probable that single courses usually provided electives.)

[41] *Ibid.*, pp. 203–204.

[42] *Ibid.*, pp. 205–206.

[43] United States Office of Education, United States Department of the Interior, Bulletin 1938, No. 6, *Offerings and Registrations in High School Subjects*, p. 1. (The nine headings obviously do not include subdivisions, but only general subject names.)

[44] *Ibid.*, p. 28.

[45] *Ibid.*, pp. 1–2.

The application of scientific study to the problems of modern life in recent years is producing an almost overwhelming body of knowledge in every area of life. A cursory survey of the development of the number of courses offered by universities and colleges over the last forty-year period will give some idea of the rate of this expansion. The organization and mastery of this steadily increasing amount of knowledge constitutes one of the most pressing problems of general education. Someone has computed the time that would be required for a student to take all of the courses offered in one of the large universities and has come to the amazing conclusion that more than a hundred years would be required for this purpose.[46]

The almost riotous growth of the curriculum and the evidences of professional dissatisfaction and confusion which appeared in the 1910's and 1920's [47] were signs that the foundations of a new curriculum had appeared. Social conditions had changed. New elements in the field of commercial and industrial education were finding an increasingly important place in the high school curriculum.[48] More and more the traditional academic disciplines had felt the impact of new interests and new demands which were to bring about important changes in the organization and content of the emerging curriculum. For instance, courses in general science appeared as early as 1905. After 1910 Stout noted an increasing number of textbooks in this field, [49] as well as the appearance of "practical" textbooks in physics, chemistry, and other science courses.[50]

[46] Homer P. Rainey, "Social Factors Affecting General Education." In *Thirty-Eighth Yearbook of the National Society for the Study of Education*, Pt. II, *General Education in the American College*, p. 17. (Guy Montrose Whipple, ed.) Public School Publishing Company, Bloomington, Ill., 1939.

[47] An interesting example is the work of the National Council of Teachers of English, which sought liberalizing reforms in the early 1910's. A good description of the background and work of this organization is to be found in the *Twenty-Sixth Yearbook of the National Society for the Study of Education*, Pt. I, pp. 43–45.

[48] Sharp increases in enrollments in vocational courses were noted in the Biennial Survey of Education, Bureau of Education, Bulletin 1924, No. 13, Vol. 1, p. 318. The National Survey of Secondary Education found industrial arts, commercial, and household arts curricula had made significant gains over a period of years. (United States Office of Education, Bulletin 1932, No. 17, Monograph No. 1, p. 169.)

[49] John Elbert Stout, *The Development of High School Curricula in the North Central States from 1860 to 1918*, pp. 236–238. The University of Chicago Press, Chicago, 1921.

[50] *Ibid.*, pp. 238–239.

Changes of a somewhat similar nature occurred in mathematics, English, and the social studies.[51]

Counts found a condition of extreme flux in the high school curriculum in the early 1920's. In a study of 90 cities over a period of five years he discovered that 341 subjects had been added to the total program, whereas 130 were abandoned. His general statement on the factors which influenced the development of the curriculum during that period is quoted as follows:

> . . . For every subject dropped almost three were added. That this condition has characterized the evolution of the high school for a half-century is suggested by the rapid expansion of its curriculum during this period. While this practice has resulted in a much needed enrichment of the narrow program of language and mathematics, it cannot be pursued indefinitely. Already the secondary-school curriculum exhibits weaknesses which may be traced to this constant addition of new materials of instruction. It is too often a mere aggregation of subjects, an unintegrated program of unrelated activities. This situation may be traced to a fundamental defect in the traditional technique of curriculum-making. A policy of *laissez-faire* has customarily been followed. The responsibility for the state of the program of studies had been neither delegated to, nor assumed by, any effective central agency. The nature of the curriculum has rather been determined by the specialists in subject matter and has been left to the mercy of the conflicts among the vested interests. Under these conditions while a new subject may be added without great opposition, the clear-cut and complete abandonment of an established subject is extremely difficult. Once it has become firmly rooted in the curriculum, unless it is the victim of violent popular passion, as in the case of German, or unless it dies of old age, as in the case of Greek, a subject is apparently able to maintain itself indefinitely. So long as a subject has friends on the high-school staff, it is relatively safe from outside attack; and, so long as a subject is taught by numerous teachers, it will not lack friends.[52]

No doubt the curricular conditions which obtained in the early 1920's could be interpreted on the basis of the extremely rapid growth of the secondary school population during that period. The "laissez faire" policy of seemingly indiscriminate

[51] *Ibid.*, pp. 228–248.

[52] George S. Counts, "Current Practices in Curriculum Making in Public High Schools." In the *Twenty-Sixth Yearbook of the National Society for the Study of Education*, Pt. I, *The Foundations and Techniques of Curriculum Construction*, pp. 139–140. (Guy Montrose Whipple, ed.) Public School Publishing Co., Bloomington, Ill., 1926.

acceptance of new courses, to which Counts refers, was probably due in large measure to the sheer expansion of the public
school movement and to the peculiarly favorable conditions of
school finance. Public high school expenditures for new buildings, grounds, and improvements were $123,576,856 in 1920, as
compared with $19,366,049 in 1910.[53] New subjects for the cur-
riculum were greeted, on the one hand, by the ramifying interests of an ever-expanding high school population, and on the
other, by a fiscal opulence which was equal to the traditional
American faith in education. It was this same bountiful support for the expanding educational program which made it
possible to maintain and even to foster some of the more traditional elements in the curriculum while new subjects were continually being added.[54]

Although the flux of curricular change in the public schools
has at times seemed chaotic, most educational innovations of
any importance can be explained in terms of changing social
demands. Traditional elements in the school program may persist long after their period of usefulness has expired, but at the
time when new elements, or subjects, come in they invariably
represent some kind of usefulness. As many educational historians have pointed out, the classical and liberal curricula of
remote periods represented a type of vocational education for
those groups which enjoyed educational privileges.

In a discussion of social pressures as affecting the American
educational program, Judd, for instance, points out that the
establishment of the land-grant colleges under the Morrill Act
was clearly an expression of a social demand for the improvement of farming through science: a demand which had arisen
out of the problem of food supply during the Civil War.[55] It was
out of this same background that later federal appropriations

[53] Federal Security Agency, United States Office of Education, Bulletin 1940,
No. 2, *Statistics of Public High Schools*, p. 11.

[54] The persistence of traditional subjects is partially explained by the fact that
college enrollments increased from 355,215 in 1910 to 597,857 in 1920. The figure
for 1930 was 1,100,737. Biennial Survey of Education, Bulletin 1937, No. 2, p. 12.
United States Office of Education, Washington, D. C., 1939.

[55] Charles H. Judd, *Education and Social Progress*, pp. 54–55. Harcourt, Brace
and Company, New York, 1934.

were applied to the development of agricultural high schools in many states.[56]

As an instance of social pressure acting on the schools, Judd cites a case in which a group of New England industrialists petitioned the Massachusetts legislature to provide for free instruction "to men, women, and children in mechanical drawing." [57] That a law making such provision was passed in 1869 is in curious contrast to the fact that drawing has sometimes been regarded as a tax-consuming luxury.

Other cases illustrating the effects of pressure groups in public education could be pointed out in considerable numbers. Judd cites the activities of casualty insurance companies in "health" education, and other groups in "temperance" education, "citizenship" education, and vocational education.[58] The immediate and powerful influences directly manifested by the pupils, themselves, are no less indicative of the force of social pressures in shaping the curriculum. It is obvious that the motives of pressure groups operating in public education are often praiseworthy and that the effects of miscellaneous pressures in the evolution of the school curriculum are not necessarily bad, or good. The curriculum must respond to social change in some way. Judd's comment in this connection is worth noting:

> . . . If there is an expansion of social interests, there will be a corresponding expansion of the curriculum. . . . The changes in the curriculum which have taken place in recent years have been dictated by many and diverse interests. These changes are, as a consequence, miscellaneous in character and uncoordinated in purpose. . . . If the schools of the future are to have a curriculum which can be relied on to give young people a well-ordered education, propaganda and domination by well-meaning but narrow-minded groups must give place to careful planning based on scientific study of social needs.[59]

The question to be raised with regard to the effects of social pressures in the development of the public school program is not how to eliminate the activities of pressure groups but how

[56] *Ibid.*, p. 57.
[57] *Ibid.*, pp. 58–59.
[58] *Ibid.*, pp. 65–82.
[59] *Ibid.*, p. 82.

to guide and coordinate changing social forces on the basis of inclusive and democratic planning.

Perhaps the most pregnant influences in the career of the modern secondary school have been those which led to the development of vocational education. Here, again, the effects of organized pressure groups are quite evident. Between 1900 and 1910 a number of organizations, including the National Association of Manufacturers, the National Metal Trades Association, certain agricultural organizations, the American Federation of Labor, and the National Education Association, had all begun to advocate extended facilities for vocational education in the public schools.[60] In 1906 a group of educators and manufacturers formed the National Society for the Promotion of Industrial Education. Their vigorous efforts over a period of years were expressive of the changing industrial and social conditions which led to the Smith-Hughes legislation and the introduction of federally supported industrial trade training in the public schools.[61]

The record of the development of federally aided vocational education in the United States since 1917 is in some respects an impressive one. On the other hand, the persistent question of the relation of vocational education to the "academic" program is one which may well be taken as the basis of an appraisal of the contemporary high school in the light of the educational demands of our changing industrial society. The actual numerical extent of vocational education will be discussed at a later point.

"General" and "Vocational" Education

The problem of the relation of vocational-industrial education to the "general" program of the schools had arisen in connection with state programs of vocational education some time before the passage of the Smith-Hughes Act in 1917.

[60] John Dale Russell and Associates, *Vocational Education*, p. 16. Prepared for the Advisory Committee on Education. United States Government Printing Office, Washington, D. C., 1938.
[61] The Smith-Hughes Act also provided for agricultural training and for instruction in home economics.

In 1915, for instance, Dewey entered a discussion of a bill proposing "dual" control of vocational education in the state of Illinois. The issue of "dual" or "unitary" control was, as Dewey stated it, "whether a sharp line of cleavage shall be drawn as respects administrative control, studies, methods and personal associations of pupils, between schools of the traditional literary type and schools of the trade-preparatory type." The effects of such a division would mean, Dewey said, "that the forces which are even now effecting a readaptation of the traditional curriculum of the elementary and high school to meet the change of social conditions, are to be driven into a narrow channel, while the old curriculum is to be left frozen in its narrow form." [62]

It must be remembered that changing conditions had brought within the scope of secondary education functions which had hitherto been performed by the family, the apprentice shop, the private trade school, and the industrial corporation. The problem was whether, under changing economic conditions, these new educational functions could be absorbed by the unitary public school. The problem was also whether the public school could maintain the integrity of its democratic spirit in the face of new and far-reaching demands.

Discussing the same problem of vocational and "general" education in 1917, Dewey pointed out that,

. . . to understand the *educational* issue is to see what difference is made in the schools themselves according as we take the *improving* of economic conditions to be the purpose of vocational training, or take its purpose to be supplying a better grade of labor for the present scheme. . . . [63]

Again raising the question of dual or unitary control, Dewey asserted that,

. . . Those who wish, whether they wish it knowingly or unknowingly, an education which will enable employees to fit better into the existing economic scheme will strive for a dual or divided system of administration. That is to say, they will attempt to have a

[62] John Dewey, "Splitting Up the School System," *New Republic*, Vol. 2, No. 24, p. 284, April 17, 1915.
[63] John Dewey, "Learning to Earn: The Place of Vocational Education in a Comprehensive Scheme of Public Education," *School and Society*, Vol. 5, No. 117, p. 332, March 24, 1917.

separate system of funds, of supervisory authorities, and, as far as possible, of schools to carry on industrial education. If they don't go as far as this, they will at least constantly harp on the difference between a liberal or cultural and a money-earning education, and will endeavor to narrow the latter down to those forms of industrial skill which will enable the future workers to fall docilely into the subordinate ranks of the industrial army.[64]

Those who wish such a kind of vocational education, Dewey said, will stress a narrow trade training, will neglect such general subjects as history and civics, will emphasize routine and drill, and will think of guidance in terms of vocational placement, alone, rather than the full realization of the peculiar capacities of each individual.[65] Dewey concluded that, ". . . The real issue is not the question whether an industrial education is to be added on to a more or less mythical cultural elementary education, but what sort of an industrial education we are to have." [66] (He held that the existing elementary school was actually vocational in character but that it stood for a restricted type of clerical training which was charged with non-democratic implications.)

In reference to the Smith-Hughes Act which had just been passed, Dewey expressed concern over the fact that the original bill which had specified unitary control had been modified to make the dual type of control optional with each state. His comment on the vocational education legislation is most significant:

. . . It settles no problem; it merely symbolizes the inauguration of a conflict between irreconcilably opposed educational and industrial ideals. Nothing is so necessary as that public-spirited representatives of the public educational interest . . . shall perceive the nature of the issue and throw their weights in municipal, state and federal educational matters, upon the side of education rather than of training, on that of democratic rather than that of feudal control of industry.[67]

Without going into a detailed consideration of the administrative control of federally aided vocational education, one may

[64] *Ibid.*, p. 333.
[65] *Ibid.*, pp. 334–335.
[66] *Ibid.*, p. 334.
[67] *Ibid.*, p. 335.

cite a number of indications of continuing tendencies toward the separation of vocational training from the traditional public school program. The limited extent of vocational education is in itself one of the most significant indexes of the gap which still separates "vocational training" from the "academic" program. Enrollments in federally aided vocational education courses have greatly increased since 1918. The enrollment figure for students in federally aided all-day classes in vocational education in agriculture, in trades and industries, and home economics, in 1937, for instance, was 591,131. This is in striking contrast to the corresponding figure of 42,485 for 1918, or 211,571 for 1928.[68] As late as 1934, however, the enrollment in federally reimbursed classes in public high schools in the 48 states constituted only 7.7 per cent of the total enrollment in such schools.[69] In 1930 only 4.6 per cent of the total number of urban boys 15 to 18 years of age were enrolled in vocational subjects in federally aided schools or classes. The proportion of rural boys in agricultural training courses was higher—13 per cent.[70] But on the whole, it is clear that only a small proportion of those pupils attending day high schools were enrolled in "vocational" courses.

Enrollments in federally aided part-time and evening classes run somewhat higher than "vocational" enrollments of regular day students in the high schools, and also affect a large group of high school age who have left school for employment. For out-of-school youth, as for those who remain in the schools, the important question is whether "vocational" education is an intrinsic function of a more inclusive program of public education. The development of publicly supported educational functions outside the schools raises difficult and embarrassing questions with respect to the function of the unitary public school.

In the report to the Advisory Committee on Education it was pointed out that the idea of "vocational" and "general" education as "two entirely distinct and separate things" has been

[68] Russell, *op. cit.*, p. 115.
[69] *Ibid.*, p. 116.
[70] *Ibid.*, p. 117.

vigorously promoted, and that the adoption of a narrow definition of vocational education "has tended to distort the whole
concept of the type of instruction that is suitable as preparation
for useful employment." [71] A further statement from the report
is pertinent at this point:

> The program in vocational education has to some extent disre-
> garded this American ideal of a single system of schools, and has
> encouraged the creation of a dual or separate school system for the
> education of workers. Stated in plainest terms, the concept behind
> the program of vocational education would segregate the young
> people who are to become industrial workers from those who are to
> go into the professions and other scholarly pursuits, and would pro-
> vide separate school facilities for these two groups. In the case of
> agriculture, it is usually necessary, because of the small school units
> that are typical of rural areas, to give the vocational courses in the
> regular high schools; but even in such cases there seems to be a de-
> liberate attempt to keep the vocational work as separate as possible
> from the other phases of the educational program. [72]

The Persistence of the College Preparatory Function

It has been suggested that the rise of "vocational" education
left the traditional high school program largely undisturbed.
The explanation of this fact requires a brief review of the
secondary school as a "college-preparatory" institution.

The twofold aim of secondary education as preparation for
college and preparation for life had been established, it will be
recalled, at the very beginning of the public high school movement. In the latter years of the nineteenth century the unitary
public school had come more and more to symbolize the open
door to college education, to personal advancement and "success." This conception of the public school was supported by
conditions which were favorable to social mobility, a large
supply of foreign labor, rapidly increasing college enrollments,
and a sharp demand for professional and white-collar workers. [73]
There was, on the other hand, the persistent fact that a large
proportion of high school students did not go on to college.

[71] Ibid., p. 129.
[72] Ibid., p. 129.
[73] Edward L. Thorndike and Percival M. Symonds, "Occupations of High
School Graduates and Non-Graduates," School Review, Vol. 30, pp. 443–451,
January, 1922.

Kandel points out that that last decade of the nineteenth century was a period of "unrest" in secondary education.[74] The functions of the secondary school were expanding. A number of short-term courses varying in length from ten to fourteen weeks had come into the curriculum. The elective system was advancing in the high schools. There were standards for college admission but they varied in different parts of the country.

In view of the general confusion the National Education Association appointed the Committee of Ten on Secondary School Studies in 1892, under the chairmanship of President Charles W. Eliot of Harvard University. The historic report of the Committee of Ten appeared in 1893. The main facts concerning the Committee and its recommendations are well known. Some indication of the motives which dominated the report is given in the fact that the Committee and the personnel of the nine subject conferences were made up largely of college presidents, professors, and school administrators—the latter actually in the minority. It seems that the curriculum was considered primarily from the standpoint of administrative problems, of which college entrance was an important one.

Nine conferences were set up on the basis of subject divisions, the tacit assumption being that the subjects, themselves, and the general organization of the curriculum, were not objects of investigation. The deliberations of the several conferences yielded a list of subjects which were to be considered proper or standard for the secondary schools, and all of the subjects were accorded equal status in the curriculum. (All subjects within the tacitly approved list were to be accepted on the grounds of their commonly disciplinary value.) In order to establish the uniformity which the equality of subjects seemed to require, a time basis was adopted which was to assure adequate training within subjects and at least approximate equivalence of training among them. Assuming the subject matter limits within which the Committee pursued its investigation, the principle of equivalence in school studies was applied to college entrance requirements. The recommendation which grew out of that line

---

[74] Kandel, *op. cit.*, p. 471.

of reasoning was, for that time, at least, a liberal one:

> . . . A college might say,—We will accept for admission any groups of studies taken from the secondary school programme, provided that the sum of the studies in each of the four years amounts to sixteen, or eighteen, or twenty periods a week,—as may be thought best,—and provided, further, that in each year at least four of the subjects presented shall have been pursued at least three periods a week, and that at least three of the subjects shall have been pursued three years or more. For the purposes of this reckoning, natural history, geography, meteorology, and astronomy might be grouped together as one subject. Every youth who entered college would have spent four years in studying a few subjects thoroughly; and on the theory that all the subjects are to be considered equivalent in educational rank for the purposes of admission to college, it would make no difference which subjects he had chosen from the programme—he would have had four years of strong and effective mental training. . . .[75]

On the more general question of the function of secondary education the Committee at least expressed the position that the main purpose of the high school is to prepare for life:

> The secondary schools of the United States, taken as a whole, do not exist for the purpose of preparing boys and girls for colleges. Only an insignificant percentage of the graduates of these schools go to colleges or scientific schools. . . . A secondary school programme intended for national use must therefore be made for those children whose education is not to be pursued beyond the secondary school. The preparation of a few pupils for college or scientific school should in the ordinary school be the incidental, and not the principal object. . . .[76]

The position of the Committee of Ten was, in effect: the same curriculum prepares for college and for "life." The same subjects were found to be equally good for all students regardless of their destination. "Equality" of subjects was obviously a reiteration of the American tradition of equality of educational opportunity. It was also the hallmark of the traditional college preparation: the Committee of Ten no doubt did much to establish the pattern of college entrance requirements for many years to come. But the pronouncement of "equality" among

---

[75] National Education Association, *Report of the Committee of Ten on Secondary School Studies*, pp. 52–53. American Book Company, New York, 1894.
[76] *Ibid.*, pp. 51–52.

subjects was also the basis of an expanding and changing curriculum.[77] It was the open door to new subjects.

The proliferation of school studies which occurred in the forty years following the report of the Committee of Ten presents a striking contrast to the fixity of certain academic patterns which persisted throughout the same period. Anyone who is familiar with the high school program of the twenties will find a familiar ring in many of the passages of the report of the Committee on College Entrance Requirements which appeared in 1899.[78] The recommended readings for English courses, for instance, include the well-known *Ivanhoe, Merchant of Venice, Last of the Mohicans, Lady of the Lake, Silas Marner,* and others which were studied by most high school students of the twenties, if not by a vast majority in very recent years.[79] High school science courses today ordinarily include biology, physics, and chemistry, in that order, and this again corresponds exactly to the pattern which was recommended by the Committee on College Entrance Requirements in 1899.[80]

There are other striking similarities between the high school curriculum of 1890 and that which millions of American youth know today. Algebra and geometry were almost universal. "General" history, civil government or civics, composition and rhetoric, Latin, bookkeeping: all of these were widely included in the curriculum of that time. Even the pattern of "first," "second," "third," and "fourth year" English had appeared, and was gaining in popularity.[81] Here and there a few subjects such as etymology and "mental philosophy" held on from an earlier period, but these anachronisms were gradually to be

[77] Kandel, *op. cit.*, pp. 484–485.

[78] National Education Association, *Report of the Committee on College Entrance Requirements.* The University of Chicago Press, Chicago, 1899. (The Committee was appointed by the National Education Association in 1895 to consider the "Requirements" problem from the standpoint of the colleges.)

[79] *Ibid.*, pp. 18, 19.

[80] *Ibid.*, p. 23. "Physical geography" was recommended for the freshman year as contrasted with the more recent "general science" which Stout dates from about 1905.

[81] John Elbert Stout, *The Development of High-School Curricula in the North Central States from 1860 to 1918,* Chap. V and VI. The University of Chicago Press, 1921.

eliminated from the secondary school program. The new commercial subjects of stenography and typewriting were found in widely scattered cases, while a few older commercial subjects such as commercial law and commercial arithmetic had started to show a definite increase. Courses in manual training had just begun to appear.[82]

The "new" subjects have increased, of course, but the dominant pattern now, as in 1890, is the college preparatory curriculum.[83] In the meantime, astronomical increases in secondary school attendance, the mounting proportion of students who do not go on to college, and the manifold problems suggested by the term "youth employment" have become matters of wide concern to educators and others who consider the problem of universal secondary education.

The Youth Work Agencies and the Public Schools

The youth work agencies were originally established as emergency measures for work-relief. They arose out of the conditions of the depression years and were addressed to the problem of unemployed youth. The Civilian Conservation Corps and the National Youth Administration were established in 1933 and 1935, respectively. Both agencies assumed educational functions, a wide-scale program having been set up in the Civilian Conservation Corps shortly after its beginning in 1933. By 1938 Congress had given explicit statutory recognition to the educational functions of the youth work agencies.[84] It appears significant that they were set up on a "relief" basis, that they assumed an educational function, and that thus far it has not been possible to separate the two phases.

Some educators consider that the youth work agencies have

[82] *Ibid.*, pp. 71–74. Stout found that about 5 per cent of a representative group of high schools in the North Central States offered courses in manual training.

[83] For a graphic description of the contemporary high school curriculum, see Herbert G. Espy, *The Public Secondary School: A Critical Analysis of Secondary Education in the United States*, pp. 4–11. Houghton Mifflin Company, Boston, 1939.

[84] Educational Policies Commission, *The Civilian Conservation Corps, The National Youth Administration and The Public Schools*, pp. 12–13. National Education Association of the United States and the American Association of School Administrators, Washington, D. C., 1941.

encroached upon the domain of the public schools. One group has taken the position that the Civilian Conservation Corps and the National Youth Administration have useful functions to perform, but that these functions are of two distinct types: one having to do with providing jobs on public works, the other with education. The one function, it is held, is that of the federal government, and should be carried out by the appropriate federal agencies, such as the U. S. Forest Service. The other function, education, is that of the public schools and should be carried out entirely under the auspices of the state and local educational agencies.[85] This, in general, is the position which was set forth by the Educational Policies Commission in 1941. The Commission also held, it should be added, that the federal government should provide such leadership and support as may be needed to establish necessary educational services and to equalize educational opportunities in the public schools.[86]

A somewhat different position was set forth in the General Report of the American Youth Commission in 1942.[87] This report, unlike that of the Educational Policies Commission, advocates the continuance of the youth work agencies with at least some of their present educational functions under the federal government. In the case of the Civilian Conservation Corps it is pointed out that it would be very difficult, if not impossible, to transfer the educational program of the camps, which are often located in isolated areas, to public school units with adequate facilities. The problem with respect to the National Youth Administration is more complex, but in this case the Report states that an important phase of the educational program has developed in connection with a number of "training centers" [88] which have an interstate function in connection

[85] *Ibid.*

[86] *Ibid.*, pp. 73–74.

[87] General Report of the American Youth Commission, *Youth and the Future,* American Council on Education, Washington, D. C., 1942.

[88] The resident work and training centers were first established in 1937 for unemployed rural youth who were brought to such "centers" for instruction in agriculture and home economics. Later the work of the centers was extended to include training in mechanical occupations and crafts. Recently the "centers" have been utilized in connection with industrial training for war industries. *Ibid.*, pp. 67 ff.

with the needs of migratory groups. Such interstate functions, it is stated, fall properly within the province of the federal government.

Accordingly, the Commission is convinced that resident work and training centers which participate in the planned interstate migration of youth should remain under the administration of the federal government. This conclusion may be based upon a new principle of federal-state relations in the fields of education and occupational adjustment, but the Commission is unable to discover any impropriety in such a principle.[89]

The position of the Report of the American Youth Commission might be summed up as a defense of the youth work agencies plus the claim that certain necessary educational functions carried on by the agencies cannot properly be assumed by the state and local educational authorities as constituted at the present time. If such a position is valid it is obvious that the public schools have been brought to something of an impasse. A new and serious challenge has been offered to the traditional American ideal of one school for all the children of all the people.

Is the "Youth Problem" an Educational Problem?

The challenge to the American public school can be examined from another standpoint. The federal youth work agencies have "encroached" upon the domain of the public schools, or "stepped into the breach" in education, according to one's point of view. On the other hand, an increasing number of American educators have become concerned over the problems of American youth. A new literature has been developed around the subject of the "youth problem," and the concept of "needs" has become a byword in education.

The educational implications of the "youth problem" are still far from clear. During the depression years the numbers of out-of-school and unemployed youth were quoted in the millions, some estimates running as high as 6,000,000. In 1937 the special census of employment and unemployed gave the figure for unemployed youth between 16 and 24 years of age, inclusive,

[89] *Ibid.*, p. 70.

as 4,000,000. The problem of youth unemployment and its associated evils is modified by the conditions of war, but many observers recognize that it may return, perhaps in an aggravated form, unless conditions are greatly altered at the conclusion of the present war. What, then, are the implications for public education and for secondary education in particular?

The question might be asked: To what extent are the public schools responsible for youth welfare? More and more, American educators have become impressed with the difficulty of drawing a line between educational responsibility and responsibility for the conditions which make for effective equality of educational opportunity. The point is illustrated by the following statement from a recent publication of the Educational Policies Commission:

. . . There must . . . be nationwide reconstruction of educational programs, in an effort more adequately to meet the needs of youth. If school officials are to have full responsibility for the operation and control of all education for youth, they are obligated to provide educational services suited to *all youth.* This obligation is not reduced if a youth withdraws from formal school before he is equipped for full-time employment. There will be no "out-of-school unemployed youth" for federal agencies to educate, when schools everywhere extend their responsibilities to all young people until they are satisfactorily established in adult vocations.[90]

The obligation of the schools to effect the placement of young workers in full-time jobs suited to their abilities is now recognized by many.[91] Those who take such a position have, in effect, pledged the schools to bridge the gap that now exists between formal education and employment. What does such an obligation entail? And where does it end?

The local school units obviously cannot undertake to meet the tremendous burdens involved in the "youth problem." It will be noted that the Educational Policies Commission did not advocate that the *functions* of the youth work agencies should be stopped. The argument in the report on the youth work agencies was that student aid, prior to the induction of the young worker into his proper occupation, should be ad-

[90] Educational Policies Commission, *op. cit.,* p. 56.
[91] *Ibid.,* p. 64.

ministrated under an inclusive program of public education in which incidental part-time employment would be controlled by broad educational purposes. The Commission also suggested that the continuance of the present federal educational agencies would result in "cleavage along class lines." [92] This observation is a significant commentary on the recent pre-war situation. It is not entirely clear, however, that the administration of "student aid" funds by state and local educational authorities would alter in any fundamental way the cleavage that already exists in the public schools as regards the vocational education program and the traditional "academic" curriculum. On the grounds of the present evidence there seems to be little indication that the existence of the federal youth work agencies has been, in and of itself, the exclusive source of the present difficulty. Whether the effects of the agencies are good or bad, they were evidently prompted by conditions which would outlast the reorganization of the administration of their functions. Without raising the question of responsibility, it appears that the "youth problem" is as wide as the social and intellectual conditions which lie at the roots of the present difficulties in secondary education in the United States. [93]

Summary

In contrast to the European socio-educational situation, the unique industrial, social, and political conditions of American life led to the development of the unitary public school. The American common school took form in a period of great industrial expansion. It provided the necessary formal literacy for a modern industrial voting population. Beyond this, its main function was that of an educational high-road to personal advancement and "success." Whatever deficiencies this conception of education may have had were disguised by the promise of the open frontier and the abundant resources of an expand-

[92] *Ibid.,* p. 78.

[93] This discussion, obviously, does not attempt to take into account the present conditions of war which have practically obliterated youth unemployment, and transformed the parallel problems of education. It assumes, however, that the social and intellectual foundations of the "youth problem" will, in some measure, persist after the present military conflict.

ing economy. There were some who questioned the assumptions upon which the American school system was built. Beard quotes Horace Greeley as asking: "To the child daily sent out from a rickety hovel or miserable garret to wrestle with Poverty and Misery for such knowledge as the teacher can impart, what true idea or purpose of Education is possible?" To this Beard adds that "even Greeley came to regard free homesteads as the escape from poverty," and that he finally conceded to the educators the argument that by land and education combined America could truly be made the home of opportunity.[94]

A combination of factors, including population changes, the continuing industrialization and urbanization of American life, and a rising standard of living combined with technological and economic factors which gradually changed the character of employment and economic opportunity, led to the vertical extension of the common school and the great development of secondary education following 1890. The main development of the secondary school took place partly as a logical development of the American conception of democratic education, partly as a result of abundance and prosperity, and partly because of economic failure and contraction. The program of studies was based on the traditional college preparatory curriculum.

As the masses of American youth entered the secondary school the curriculum expanded, non-academic subjects came in, and a program of federally aided vocational education was set up. Vocational education, however, is still by and large an "outsider" in the public school program. The college preparatory curriculum continues to be the dominating pattern of secondary education. During the transition from a selective institution to a popular one the high school changed, but its changes were not commensurate to the demands of its changing population. Moreover, there is much evidence to show that such changes as occurred were without the benefit of any broad social orientation, and were brought about largely through the

[94] Educational Policies Commission, *The Unique Function of Education in American Democracy*, p. 48. National Education Association of the United States and the Department of Superintendence, Washington, D. C., 1937.

exercise of pressures, rather than by any comprehensive plan.

In recent years the widespread concern of educators over the "youth problem," and the appearance of the youth work agencies, has combined with other factors leading to much criticism of the secondary school, and to many attempts to reform the high school curriculum. The problem of secondary education is considered in this study as one which must be defined in terms of the social and economic conditions out of which it arose. One of the fundamental assumptions of the study is that any proposal regarding the present function of the secondary school must be judged on the basis of its effectiveness in meeting the crucial socio-educational problems that now confront the secondary school.

The unitary common school system of the United States was based upon American democracy and the promise of an abundant life for all the people. The present crisis in secondary education cannot be considered apart from the social conditions upon which it rests.

CHAPTER II

THE NEW EDUCATION IN THE SECONDARY SCHOOLS

THE PURPOSE of this chapter is to review certain phases of the Progressive movement as a major development in American secondary education, and to appraise some of its possible strengths and weaknesses in relation to the present high school program. Subsequent chapters will deal with certain other challenging conceptions and tendencies in American education, which may be considered of strategic importance to the secondary school and its function in American life, as viewed by the writer. His position is summed up, positively, in the final chapter.

Progressive educators turned to the secondary school in the early 1930's. Directing their attack to the traditional "subject" curriculum of the college preparatory school, they sought to apply the activity concept and the principles of the child-centered education to the secondary curriculum. Also evident in the Progressive movement was a strong tendency to take into account the social function of the public school; in fact, it was often argued that an activity school was inherently centered in the normal social setting of pupil activities. Whether the Progressive group in American education has developed an effective answer to the secondary school problem is the subject of the present chapter of this study. It must be recognized at the outset, of course, that there is no single well-defined position which is *the* Progressive position. There are at least two rather widely divergent tendencies in "Progressivism" which must be taken into account.

During the period in which the Progressive philosophy of education was taking form in American life the secondary school continued to cling to its traditional program, as the preceding chapter has shown. To the traditional secondary school Progressive education offered revolutionary alternatives. (Many of the new conceptions were at first limited to the elementary school, so far as practice was concerned at least, but at length the new education was to be applied to the secondary school, as well.)

The rise of the Progressive movement in American education, including its recent effects in the secondary schools, was based upon the liberal and scientific traditions as they took form in American life. Without making any initial assumptions regarding the internal consistency of that rather complex body of ideas and practices which have been associated with the term "Progressive education," it is clear that at least certain common roots of the "New" education may be identified. Among its central conceptions were those of the democratic emphasis on the primacy of the individual, and the scientific method with its emphasis on the authority of the experimentally determined fact. Also strongly influential in the Progressive movement was a new conception of man and nature in which pragmatic experimentalism [1] sought to combine the democratic philosophy with the scientific attitude by locating authority in empirical events, which were to be accepted and studied in terms of their own emergent qualities. This view, which was common to pragmatism and Progressive education, was based on an evolutionary conception of man as continuous with nature (including the social environment). It also stood for a fundamental emphasis on man's disposition to improve his lot, and the respective values of science and democracy in his endeavors to do so.

Progressive education, like the philosophy of experimentalism, was an indigenous product of American life, but it was not without its European antecedents. Its ideas have been traced back to such names as Rousseau, Pestalozzi, Herbart, Froebel, and beyond them to antiquity. The following statements, for instance, are found in *The Republic*:

[1] The educational implications of pragmatism are discussed by John L. Childs, in *Education and the Philosophy of Experimentalism*. D. Appleton-Century Company, New York, 1931.

. . . A freeman ought not to be a slave in the acquisition of knowledge of any kind. . . . Knowledge which is acquired under compulsion obtains no hold on the mind.

. . . Do not use compulsion, but let early education be a sort of amusement; you will then be better able to find out the natural bent.[2]

In all probability, some of the "modern" educational ideas took their rise with the very beginnings of formal education, i.e., just as soon as it became possible to distinguish between "everyday life" activities and those organized "school" activities which represent adult conceptions of what children ought to learn. At least, the stage of civilization at which a deliberate program of instruction is set up (and for whatever group) suggests the strong possibility that competing social movements would somehow help to crystallize divergent conceptions of curriculum content which tend to fall back upon methodological arguments having to do with its selection, organization, and presentation. At this point one would expect to find the ascending, challenging, or critical groups in the society conjoined, however vaguely and implicitly, with educational attempts to dislodge conventional subject matters and to inaugurate a new curriculum through the substitution of new interests. It was the same Rousseau who wrote *Emile* and the *Social Contract* and it was the same Dewey who wrote *Democracy and Education* and *Liberalism and Social Action*. It is not without significance that a good share of the philosophers and great social critics made important contributions to educational theory, and sometimes immediate contributions to practice, as well.

The Challenge to the Traditional School

Perhaps the primary challenge of Progressive education to the traditional school was a new conception of learning. Based upon a behavioral psychology, which viewed the organism and environment as continuous, the active conception of learning was first of all cognizant of the educational significance of the complete range of behavior, including its overt, physical aspects. In

[2] From *The Republic,* in *The Works of Plato.* (Translation by B. Jowett), p. 297. The Dial Press, New York.

its minimal, biological sense, it was opposed to passive listening, to the restraint of normal physical activity, including the manipulation of environmental materials, and to all the manifold implications of the notion that "the individual child is an isolated unit so completely self-enclosed that he can be treated entirely apart from the environment which actually penetrates his every act and thought." [3] Implicit in the conception of learning as active was the idea of purposive, self-initiated activity, which was a challenge to dictated or imposed activities of all kinds.

In its full meaning the active conception of learning was considered as the complete, purposive act, or the "complete act of thought." [4] This was the foundation of Kilpatrick's formulation of the "project method," [5] which became so widely influential in the new education. The active conception of learning, in the full sense, was opposed to partial, fragmentary, and meaningless "learnings" of all kinds. It challenged the page-to-page assignment and the imposed drill activity isolated from the normal activity which involved the exercise of the skill. It was a challenge to the "subject" organization of the curriculum, and as such it inaugurated the search for a more satisfactory type of organization for the school program.

The meaning of learning as active was summed up in the "complete act of thought," but the Progressive view of education also required a *continuity* of activities, each leading to progressively larger and more satisfactory experiences. Inherent in its concept of *"growth"* was the important principle that ends were developed out of the life process, and not imposed from without.[6] In view of the "growth" principle, the new education was opposed to compartmentalized and "closed-in" activities, to the

<hr>

[3] John L. Childs, *Education and the Philosophy of Experimentalism*, p. 71. D. Appleton-Century Company, New York, 1931.

[4] For a definitive discussion of this concept, see John Dewey, *How We Think*.

[5] William H. Kilpatrick, *The Project Method: The Use of the Purposeful Act in the Educative Process*. Bureau of Publications, Teachers College, Columbia University, New York, 1921. (Reprint from *Teachers College Record*, September, 1918.)

[6] John Dewey, *Democracy and Education*, especially Chap. IV. The Macmillan Company, New York, 1916.

"subject" required-of-all, to the dual system of "general education" and college preparation on the one hand, and the various
types of specific trade training on the other. It was also opposed
to the imposition of beliefs and attitudes: education was to
teach *how* to think, not *what* to think.

In practice, the principle of "growth" offered such alternatives as exploratory courses, guidance based not on a limited
conception of placement but on the attempt to discover the
capacities of each individual and aid in their development. The
principle of growth opposed to the curriculum composed of
"subjects" the conception of a more flexible school in which a
new method and a new type of "psychological" organization of
materials would overcome the frustrating and coercive effects of
subject-dominated activities leading to fixed ends or to imposed
beliefs.

A third, fundamental conception of Progressive education
(which was also coordinate to the principles of "active learning"
and "growth") was that of the social character of the educative
process. Truly revolutionary was the idea that *normal human
activities were educative,* that the school was actually a part of
the community life and not an isolated social hatchery in which
pupils were to be imbued with a kind of knowledge which was
somehow prior to experience. Intimately connected with this
view were two equally important corollaries: first, that the community, as the normal setting of human activities, was the
fundamental educative unit; and second, that the formal school
was a partial and deliberate educational enterprise within an
inclusive framework of cultural evolution.

The foregoing conceptions were opposed to the traditional
school of alphabetically differentiated pupil units, fixed chairs,
uniform assignments, individual and almost secretive study,
competitive marking, and the general preoccupation with
knowledge for its own sake.

In terms of the new conception of the social character of the
school, group activities (utilizing the unique interests and
capacities of individuals) were to be organized, carried out, and
evaluated, on the basis of cooperative group planning. The

activities of the school were to be as lifelike as possible. They
were to express an integral relationship between the school and
the community, and to be dedicated to the fundamental purposes of the larger society—to democracy and the welfare of
the American people. Democracy as a way of life was to be
practiced and cultivated within the school.

The Progressive Movement

The general effects of the Progressive movement in American
education are too well known to require a detailed account.
Until about 1930 the main development of the new education
was limited to the elementary schools, but after that time the
high schools became more and more responsive to the activity
principle and to other Progressive conceptions which for many
educators seemed to hold the possible answer to a critical educational problem. From the beginning, however, it was clear that
in the secondary schools the new education was faced with added
difficulties and with conditions different in many respects from
those in elementary education.

Particular attention should be given to the fact that the "new"
education was first developed at the elementary level. The
early experimental schools which fed into the movement later
known as "Progressive" were developed on the basis of protest
against the formalism and rigid disciplinary conception of
learning in the traditional school. They were the work of
educational pioneers and reformers who conceived of education
as growth, and who sought to provide a setting in which materials and methods could be better adapted to the normal activities of children. Such was the purpose of Dewey's Laboratory School which was founded at Chicago in 1896.

Dewey's experimental school is of peculiar significance, not
only because it stood for the general principles of the activity
school but also because it was a deliberate attempt to base an
educational program on the peculiar conditions of this in-
dustrial-democratic society.

The main purposes of Dewey's Laboratory School were probably best described by his statement in *School and Society*,

which was first published in 1900.[7] Proceeding on the initial
assumption that movements in education should be related to
the broad, social view, Dewey's interpretation of the "New Education" was made in the light of changing social and industrial
conditions.

He found the industrial revolution and its effects to have excluded children from the normal forms of social and economic
participation which belonged to the earlier period when production was carried on largely in home and neighborhood units.
Important educational values connected with responsible participation of children in the productive activities of the community had been lost. There were compensations, to be sure,
but the school had found its traditional program less and less
suited to the needs of pupils who were literally divorced from
the community life. The problem, therefore, was to restore to
education the sense of reality and responsibility which accom-
panies the normal activities of the social group.

Dewey observed the introduction of new courses in manual
and household arts which he found to be signs of the times, but
the "New Education" was to be much more than "vocational"
or "technical" in the narrow sense of these words. "Occupational education" was Dewey's term, and this was used to de-
note a school in which children would actually engage in types
of useful activities as carried on by adults in an industrial society. The purposeful activities of real life were to comprise
the "instrumentalities through which the school itself shall be
made a genuine form of active community life, instead of a
place set apart in which to learn lessons."[8] In such a school, activities were to be organized on lines of common purpose.
Natural conditions were to be set up for the interchange of
thought and for the expression and enlargement of common
feelings. The school subjects under such conditions would
take on new meaning and vitality, for they would be actually
joined to the normal social medium in which they were developed.

[7] John Dewey, *The School and Society.* The University of Chicago Press,
Chicago, 1900.
[8] *Ibid.,* p. 27.

From the general development of the early laboratory schools it appears that their efforts were characterized chiefly by an emphasis on child growth which was generally considered primarily from the standpoint of the more immediate home-school environment of the pupil. The early phase of the Progressive movement in American education has been significantly described as the development of the "Pupil-centered school." In recent years, particularly, the earlier emphasis on child growth, per se, has been modified by an increasing degree of concern for environmental influences as they affect the problems of education. The general character of this change is summed up in the following quotation from a statement issued by the Progressive Education Association:

The serious social-economic crises of recent years have had a profound effect upon education, arousing educators all over the country to a consciousness of their obligation to work for the removal of the economic and social barriers to educational opportunity for a greater number of children. This has been reflected in the Association in a shift of emphasis, both in the conference and in the magazine, from the problems of child growth, which occupied the attention of members in the earlier days, to consideration of the crucial questions of our economic and social life.[9]

The foregoing paragraph appears to be warranted in so far as it indicates a general shift in the attitudes of Progressive and other American educators. However, there has been, and there continues to be, considerable diversity and some confusion among Progressive educators with regard to both practice and theory. The differences at times appear to be highly significant. Certainly, they have been emphasized by important social changes which throw new light on the discussion of problems having to do with educational content and method. It is of added interest that the organized resources of the "new" education were first applied to the problem of the secondary school curriculum just at the time when this "transition" in American education had begun to gather momentum.

[9] Progressive Education Association, *Progressive Education Advances*, pp. 8–9. D. Appleton-Century Company, New York, 1938.

Progressivism in Secondary Education

In 1929, the year preceding the establishment of the Commission on the Relation of School and College, the National
Education Association issued a research bulletin called *Vitalizing the School Curriculum*. This publication reported a study
in which twenty-six "experts" had been polled on "helpful
books dealing with high school curriculum problems." Each
"expert" submitted six titles which were ultimately compiled
in a list. The first six books of the list, in order of preference,
included: Bobbitt, *How to Make a Curriculum;* Uhl, *Secondary School Curricula;* Williams, *The Making of High School
Curricula;* Charters, *Curriculum Construction;* and the *Fifth*
and *Sixth Yearbooks of the Department of Superintendence* on
the junior high school, and the high school curriculum, respectively.[10] The most striking characteristic of these books was
their predominantly technical and "scientific" emphasis. "Differentiation" was the order of the day. "Quantitative" research
studies and "activity analysis" still dominated the field of curriculum planning. However, the Scientific Movement which
had featured the application of empirical, "quantitative" research methods to problems of curriculum development had
already passed its zenith.

After 1930 the case for a secondary school curriculum based
on the precepts of the new education gradually found more and
more expression in a variety of plans which were called by such
names as "correlation," "broad fields," "unified studies," "social-
living courses," "broad-fields curriculum," "integrated curriculum," "core curriculum," and the like. Although there was
much variation among these several plans, common to all of
them was the tendency to center learning in the purposes of
the learner, or at least in "areas" of experience which were
planned to reflect the common needs and problems of pupils
rather than the logic of prescribed subject matters. Taking the
"active" conception of learning as an index, some Progressive

[10] National Education Association, *Research Bulletin*, Vol. 7, No. 4, *Vitalizing
the High School Curriculum*, p. 243. Research Division of the National Education Association, Washington, D. C., 1929.

leaders arranged proposals for a new secondary program on a scale which put at one pole the traditional subject curriculum. Modifications of the traditional program were arranged along this scale in the degree to which the subjects were modified or abandoned, and all the reformed curricula were assumed to move toward the other pole, which has sometimes been called the "experience curriculum."

Without attempting a complete survey of developments, it should be useful to indicate some main recent tendencies of curriculum revision in the secondary schools as influenced by the emphases of Progressive education.

Certainly, wide-scale changes have occurred. Recent books on the curriculum and secondary education are filled with references to "promising" innovations.[11] In 1938 Aiken reported that 70 per cent of the larger cities, 50 per cent of the middle-sized cities, and 30 per cent of the smaller towns of the country were "engaged in extensive studies of the problems of secondary education."[12] It would be hazardous to assume that all of this reform activity was motivated exclusively by Progressive ideas. However, the extent of the influence of the new education is suggested by a reliable estimate that four out of five schools in America were affected in some degree by the ideas of "integration," in 1937.[13]

The Core

In the various efforts to define a more suitable type of organization for the high school curriculum, perhaps the most significant development, and certainly the best known, was that of the "core" curriculum. Since the term "core" came into common usage, it has been associated with a wide variety of curricular plans, ranging from the traditional program in which certain

[11] See: Samuel Everett (edr.), *The Changing Curriculum;* Harold Spears, *The Emerging High School Curriculum;* Harold Rugg (edr.), *Democracy and the Curriculum,* Chap. XVIII.

[12] Wilford M. Aiken, "The Commission on the Relation of School and College," *Educational Research Bulletin,* Vol. 17, No. 8, p. 218. Ohio State University, Columbus, Ohio, 1938.

[13] L. Thomas Hopkins, *Integration: Its Meaning and Application,* pp. 197–198. D. Appleton-Century Company, New York, 1937.

subjects were sometimes labeled as the "core," toward a thoroughgoing type of activity program.[14] In general, however, the "core" has represented attempts to organize the curriculum in such a way that at least some of the learning experiences of pupils would be defined by common needs and interests and developed on some other basis than that of the traditional subjects.

Perhaps the most widely influential, and probably the best known, "core" program was that which was developed in the state of Virginia. This widely publicized plan was based on the primary assumption that the "core" should reflect the common needs of pupils.

> . . . the core program is based upon needs common to all high school pupils and corresponds roughly to what were formerly known as "required" or "constant" subjects. . . .[15]

One of the major underlying principles was that Education should provide for the continuous and guided growth of boys and girls toward a life of "effective citizenship"[16] and "individual realization,"[17] and to assure this cumulative and guided growth a plan[18] was set up on the basis of a "core" of "major functions of social life" which was to serve as a basis of organization for the common "core" experiences. Also included in the plan was a careful statement of aims including "attitudes" and "appreciations" which were representative of "general characteristics of behavior exemplifying the democratic way of living."[19] The plan of "scope," however, with its set of "social functions" prescribing minimum areas of experience for the well-rounded development of effective citizens, and the optimum growth of the individual, is probably the most significant aspect of the Virginia program. The difference between

[14] Hopkins, *op. cit.*, p. 152.
[15] Virginia State Board of Education, *Public Schools in Virginia*, Bulletin, Vol. 22, No. 4, p. 23, January, 1940. Richmond, Va.
[16] *Ibid.*, p. 23.
[17] Virginia State Board of Education, *Tentative Course of Study for the Core Curriculum of Secondary Schools*, Bulletin, Vol. 17, No. 2, pp. 1–2, August, 1934. Richmond, Va.
[18] *Ibid.*, pp. 15 ff.
[19] *Ibid.*, p. 2.

the new "core" and the required subjects of the old-type curriculum is summed up in the following statement from a
state bulletin in 1939:

"The Curriculum" is defined in The Virginia Program as all of
the experiences which the pupils have while under the guidance of
the school. For many years accredited high schools in Virginia have
required sixteen units of credit for graduation, nine of which resulted from required courses. These required courses constituted the
"core" or that part of the school offering prescribed for all pupils.
The chief difference between the "core" heretofore and that recommended in the Curriculum Revision Program is the fact that the
revised program does not propose a core made up of specific subjects. It proposes that the experience which is required of all pupils
in the fields of social studies, language arts (English), and science
shall be secured through the study of social problems rather than
isolated "subjects." The revised courses of study for the core curriculum of high schools organize instruction around problems of social
significance, such as conservation, health, use of leisure, changing
standards of living, and other problems which have purpose and
meaning for the pupils.
    In the study of each problem there is always opportunity for ex-
tensive experience in language arts and social studies, and in many
problems there will be opportunity for extensive experience in
science and less often in mathematics.[20]

The widespread use of the general pattern of organization of
the "core," as consisting of "units of work" or "problems of living" to be developed within such non-subject categories as "social functions," "areas of living," etc., is abundantly illustrated
in the several state programs[21] which followed the general out-
lines of the Virginia plan, and in many single school programs
which need not be cited. Certain general tendencies in the development of the various types of core curricula, however,
should be noted.

    In 1940 Spears described a number of common characteristics
which he found in the core programs of the co-operating

[20] Virginia State Board of Education, Bulletin, Vol. 21, No. 4, p. 18, 1939.
Richmond, Va.
    [21] Bulletin No. 7, *Mississippi Program for the Improvement of Instruction,
Curriculum Reorganization in the Secondary School, Grades 7–12.* State Department of Education, Jackson, Miss., October, 1939.
    Curriculum Bulletin No. 7, *Alabama Curriculum Development Program. Plan-
ning the Core Curriculum in the Secondary School,* State of Alabama, Department of Education, Department Bulletin 1940, No. 2, 1939.

schools in California.[22] The following points are significant: "The most obvious general trend" was the "reliance upon the social studies as the integrating center around which other materials may be brought into play."

> In general, the core in the Cooperating Schools contains units in orientation for incoming pupils, a semester or a year of what may be termed "world culture," a year or more of American history—including civics and current affairs—and senior problems. Oral and written expression grow out of the problems or experiences arising from such a combination. At other times current social and economic problems, as representative of social life today, are taken as the core structure, with related experiences being drawn from those areas outside the social studies just mentioned. This tendency of the California schools to build a core from the formerly separate fields of social studies, English, art, and music—and occasionally science or mathematics—is in keeping with the practice in the other secondary schools of the country that have moved toward a core program. The most common fusion is that of social studies and English.[23]

Other significant features noted by Spears were the inclusion of orientation courses for incoming students, and the general tendency of "core" teachers to assume guidance responsibilities in connection with their teaching, general concern for the achievement of basic skills, and also some interest in the "cultivation of the social graces" by bringing the organization of school "social" activities into closer contact with the purposes of the "core."[24]

In the second volume of the report of the Eight-Year Study of the Commission on the Relation of School and College, the common elements found in the organization and administration of core courses are summed up as follows:

> Certain common elements are found upon examining the organization and administration of these core courses. First, they cut across subject-matter lines; second, they frequently call for cooperative planning and teaching; third, they call for exploration of a

[22] A group of eleven high schools in California engaged in an experimental program. Harold Spears, *The Emerging High School Program*, pp. 230–242. American Book Company, New York, 1940.
  See also: Bulletin of the California State Department of Education, *Programs of the Co-operating Schools in California*. California State Department of Education, Sacramento, May, 1939.
[23] Spears, *op. cit.*, pp. 232–233.
[24] *Ibid.*, pp. 235–239.

wide range of relationships; fourth, they provide for experiences valid for large groups; fifth, they deal with subject matter which does not require extended drill in specific skills (such as the operations involved in mathematics, or the writing of chemical equations); sixth, they use larger blocks of time than a single period; and seventh, they use a wide range of source materials, techniques of gathering information, and classroom activities.[25]

In the report from which the foregoing quotation is taken it is indicated that four general approaches to the "core" program have been developed. Without undertaking a detailed analysis of the several "approaches," it should be noted that the four types were divided into two main categories: first, "The Core Curriculum Based on Adult Needs or Social Demands," and second, "The Core Curriculum Based on Adolescent Needs."[26]

In this latter type of program the curriculum is planned "around problems arising from the personal-social interactions of the individual in the various aspects of living."[27] Broad categories of personal-social relationships are employed to guide the planning of types of activities, but great flexibility is allowed to provide for wide participation of students in planning the scope and sequence of the program. "The activities of a class followed no fixed or internally logical sequence, such as would be defined by a textbook or course of study."[28]

The contrasting tendencies of the "core" as based on "social demands" and the "core" as based on "adolescent needs" are highly significant, from the standpoint of this study. The possible implications will be discussed at a later point.

In summing up the general characteristics of the "core" development in secondary education it should first be noted that the broad-fields curriculum, the reorganized single course, or "subject," and other prominent tendencies in secondary school curriculum reorganization are all indicative, in some respects at least, of a general movement in modern education. The exact

[25] H. H. Giles, S. P. McCutchen, and A. N. Zechiel, *Exploring the Curriculum, Adventure in American Education,* Vol. 2, pp. 33–34. (Commission on the Relation of School and College of the Progressive Education Association.) Harper and Brothers, New York, 1942.

[26] *Ibid.,* pp. 32–48.

[27] *Ibid.,* p. 44.

[28] *Ibid.,* p. 45.

point at which a reaction against the traditional "subject" program becomes a "core" is not easy to determine. However, anyone who has observed the development of the various types of "core" curricula will probably recognize the following significant tendencies: "Subject" lines are generally broken down. The "core" program tends to place greater emphasis on pupil needs and interests, and to encourage pupil participation in educational planning. It is a common program for all, or nearly all, pupils. It generally entails a daily schedule in which a relatively large block of time is set apart for core activities. With rare, if any, exceptions, the core is less than the entire curriculum. The importance of the "core" concept, and its rather wide acceptance among Progressive educators have been amply illustrated.

Finally, it is noted that regardless of the "functional" categories which may be employed, "core" activities are often developed within the general range of the academic subject fields, especially "social studies," "language arts," and science. Whether the "adolescent needs" approach to the "core" actually escapes the domination of the academic tradition, and whether it provides adequate alternatives to the "subject" curriculum and also to the "social demands" type of "core" are matters for later discussion.

Limitations

The extent and character of the curricular changes which actually have been brought about by the apparently widespread interest in the "new" education would be difficult to determine with accuracy. Certainly, large numbers of school systems have given attention to the problem of revising the secondary school curriculum in recent years, as already indicated. On the other hand, any appraisal of the "modern" trend in secondary education should take into account the actual character of the changes made. In 1932 Briggs found that,

At no time, from the beginning to the present, has there been fundamental thinking that has materially affected secondary education. The history of American secondary education is chiefly a history of tradition modified slowly, and usually by factors other than a clear vision of what it should contribute to the social order. . . . Most innovations must be tacked on to the traditional program, without disturbing it very much.[29]

In 1938 the writer analyzed eighty descriptive accounts of innovating practices in high schools, taken from educational periodicals for the years 1936, 1937, and 1938. Out of the eighty articles, ten indicated some attempt to effect a fundamental reorganization of the type that would involve cutting across the usual subject matter boundaries. Of that ten, four were described as "core curricula," three as "fused" courses in English and social studies, and one as a reorganized and broadened social studies program. Seventy of the total eighty innovations could be designated as mere additions or superstructures built upon the former curricula. Suggestive of the general trend in the preponderant group of innovations were the following titles of the descriptive articles: "A Course in Consumer Education," "An Automobile Driving Plan with Novel Features," "A High School History," "Pupils Act as Teachers' Secretaries," "Boys and Girls Exchange Class Periods," "A School Newsreel," "A Course in Orientation," "Training for Parenthood at the Secondary Level." The impressions left by this sampling of the descriptive literature are confirmed in a somewhat earlier statement by J. Wayne Wrightstone, whose study of experimental high school practices led him to the following conclusion:

. . . Within recent years changes in secondary education have been restricted by traditional practices and the influence of college entrance requirements to a rather narrow and formal academic curriculum. The curricular changes that have crept into secondary schools have been additions to the existing compartments of the secondary curriculum rather than inclusive changes. The reforms have been piecemeal, partial, opportunistic, and uncoordinated with any comprehensive educational outlook or philosophy.[30]

Obviously, there were a number of distinctive conditions at the secondary school level which were to have important effects

[29] Thomas H. Briggs, "A Vision of Secondary Education," *Teachers College Record*, Vol. 34, pp. 2–3, October, 1932.
[30] J. Wayne Wrightstone, *Appraisal of Experimental High School Practices*, p. 3. Bureau of Publications, Teachers College, Columbia University, New York, 1936.

in the adaptation of progressive theories to its curriculum. Early attempts at curriculum reorganization were often addressed primarily to the reorganization of subjects, rather than pupil behavior, and with relatively few exceptions "reorganized" high school curricula in recent years were still fundamentally "subject" programs.[31] The persistence of the subjects in the face of widespread dissatisfaction and desire for curriculum reorganization may be taken as due in part to college entrance requirements—in part, perhaps, to the maturing and specializing interests of secondary school pupils. In any event the problem of subjects will be discussed later.

The Quest for More Fundamental Reorganization

It is noteworthy that some educators regarded the "core" as a transitional stage leading to a program more completely centered in the normal, daily living of pupils. When President Leigh of Bennington College made his study of the early plans which were developed by schools of the Eight Year Study he ventured the opinion that "completely to the left of these programs, there could surely be conceived a senior high school program in line with modern psychology and 'progressive' education, which in its radical approach to the problem of learning, would begin where these left off." [32] It was a similar conception which led to the development of the theory of the "experience curriculum" as stated by Hopkins and the Committee on Integration in 1937.[33]

Using the fundamental conception of the curriculum as consisting of the purposeful experiences of pupils, many educators were constantly pointing to more fundamental conceptions of reconstruction in secondary education. Briggs's early criticism of the uncoordinated and random efforts at curriculum revision has been cited.[34] In 1936, Kilpatrick asked for a type of activity

[31] L. Thomas Hopkins, *Integration: Its Meaning and Application*, pp. 259 ff. D. Appleton-Century Company, New York, 1937.

[32] Quoted by Harold Alberty, in Harold Rugg (edr.), *Democracy and the Curriculum*, p. 282. D. Appleton-Century Company, New York, 1939. (Leigh's study was made in 1933.)

[33] Hopkins, *op. cit.*, pp. 253–275.

[34] See pp. 51–52.

school at the secondary level which would enable pupils to give a good portion of their time to a "life-process" program ignoring subject divisions.[85] Kilpatrick's proposal took the position that there should be a very gradual and completely continuous transition from the activity program of the elementary school to a certain degree of specialized education based upon the individual needs of students at the high school level. The aim was "to contrive a school program that will keep education for all the pupils on a basis of living for most of each day at the beginning of the high-school period and grant the privilege of specialization only as an affirmative case is made out for each individual concerned." [36]

The Distinctive Problems of Secondary Education

Some important effects of the conceptions of active learning and growth in Progressive practice and theory in secondary education have been indicated.[37] At the same time, it is apparent that the attempts to implement the conceptions of the new education have been widely variant, often confused, and generally much less successful than in the case of elementary education. In view of the history of the Progressive Movement it appears probable that some of the difficulties in secondary education are related to the peculiar conditions of the educative process at that level.

In 1900 Dewey pointed out that changing conditions of industry, population, and employment had already resulted in the growing exclusion of the child from the normal activities of the adult community.[38]

It is probably not entirely accidental that Progressive conceptions of education were first adopted at the elementary school level. Changing economic and social conditions, particularly

[85] William Heard Kilpatrick, *Remaking the Curriculum*, p. 105. Newson and Company, New York, 1936.

[36] *Ibid.*, p. 101.

[37] A series of highly suggestive proposals for reconstruction in secondary education are contained in: Samuel Everett (edr.), *A Challenge to Secondary Education.* (Society for Curriculum Study, Committee on Secondary Education.) D. Appleton-Century Company, New York, 1935.

[38] Dewey, *op. cit.*, pp. 6 ff.

in work and the family life, no doubt helped to prepare the way for a new conception of child behavior which was expressed in the earliest attempts to reorganize elementary education at the turn of the century. Changing industrial patterns, especially the development of large-scale machine production, had by this time pretty well shifted the locus of work responsibilities to the adult end of the family scale.[39] Children were largely excluded from responsible participation in the affairs of grown-ups. Hence, they "ceased to be thought of as adults in miniature and came to be valued in their own right as children, with their own peculiar characteristics and possibilities."[40] This new conception of childhood henceforth became the basis of a new kind of elementary school "which dedicated itself to helping the child live richly and fully *as a child* in home, school, and community, on the assumption that in so doing he would best equip himself for responsible adulthood in a wider society."[41]

In similar fashion, the Commission finds that current problems in secondary education reflect the changing social and economic status of the adolescent whose exclusion from adult activities and responsibilities now requires corresponding adjustments in the high school program.[42] There can be little doubt that changing social conditions have made it increasingly difficult for youth to cross the "threshold of adulthood," and that the process of "growing-up" has been retarded because young men and women in recent pre-war times have been barred from many relationships which depend upon earning.

The full implications of this cultural ejection of the young, and especially its gradual extension into the higher age brackets, are still not entirely clear.

In the elementary school there are a number of reasons why the use of widely accepted notions of Progressive methods contributed to results which were generally regarded as successful.

[39] This factor is cited in: V. T. Thayer, Caroline Zachry, and Ruth Kotinsky, *Reorganizing Secondary Education*. (Report of the Commission on Secondary Curriculum of the Progressive Education Association), pp. 4 ff. D. Appleton-Century Company, New York, 1939.

[40] *Ibid.*, p. 4.

[41] *Ibid.*, pp. 4–5.

[42] *Ibid.*, p. 5.

To begin with, there is the relative importance of overt, physical activity in the life and growth of the young child. There can be no question, of course, regarding the altogether beneficial results of the application of Progressive ideas pertaining to the rounded development of the "whole child" in secondary education, as well, but the limitations of the simple formula for the release of normal activities at the higher age levels are only too apparent.

Of greater importance with respect to the peculiar character of elementary education is the important fact that under ordinary conditions a relatively limited environment can be controlled so as to provide an adequate medium for the early development of the child. The term "adequate" is used in the sense of meeting common expectations and widely accepted standards. It is fully recognized, of course, that even the young children of the poor and unemployed are not immune to the effects of their depressed station in society, that their home and social environment may be culturally meager, if not inadequate to their physical needs. But it is also evident that the elementary school is relatively able in its attempts to provide an environment in which the normal physical and cultural development of the child may be obtained without conspicuous failure. It should be remembered that the rapid development of children in their early years is a never-ceasing source of wonder and gratification to the adult population. Moreover, the standards of "normal" growth in the child are relatively stable and less subject to differences of interpretation which tend to develop in the case of youth.

Closely associated with the relatively powerful school environment of children is the home and its dominant influence in the life of the very young. The social environment of the child is in fact largely an extension of the home which joins with the institutionalized home-life of the school. In this home-school environment the average child carries on his daily activities in a medium which reflects but also cushions the impact of the larger community.

With respect to the child's intellectual development, much

can be gained through direct observation, the overt manipulations of objects, and the simplest forms of social intercourse so long as the immediate physical and social environment remain largely unexplored. Moreover, the problem of selection and organization of content is somewhat simplified by the fact that a good deal of this early exploration of the child's environment consists in the discovery of generalizations and conventions, i.e., simple and relatively persistent patterns of physical, intellectual, and social behavior which would become controlling factors in his experience at some time or another, in any case.

The child lives in a "common-sense" world in which most meanings are essentially clear. He learns to take for granted certain ideas, values, ways of doing things and thinking about things. As he matures, basic, cultural patterns of thought and conduct become a part of him in the sense that they are ingrained in habits whose consistently satisfying effects give no occasion to thought about the ideas and values they represent. For the very young the meanings of "up" and "down," of "good" and "bad," of "false" and "true," are absolutes. In modern society the period of childish "innocence" tends to be foreshortened. Indeed, the precocity of the modern child has long been a subject of humorous comment, but by and large the intellectual and emotional life of the pre-adolescent makes demands which are less challenging to commonly accepted standards of growth than in the case of his older brother or sister.

In the case of the beginning secondary school pupil the isolated play-world of the child has already been somewhat broken down. This process continues. Primary physical and cultural adjustments give way before more complex types of activity which involve contacts with ever larger and more remote groups. The behavior of the individual becomes continuous with that of others vastly removed in time and space. Obviously this involves more extensive communication, and the greater use of symbols as cues to present behavior.

With the coming of physiological and emotional maturity the youth requires an enlarging field for the exercise of his developing powers. The protective environment of home and school

recedes (or should recede, at least) and the youth is brought
into more direct contact with the adult community in which his
maturing interests and abilities seek expression, often with
frustrating effects.

At the same time, the world of meanings and values becomes
less clear and less certain. Many of the absolutes of childhood
are challenged and the realm of "common-sense" gives way before a world of controversy and competing ideas.

It has been suggested that the age of puberty, which brings to
the individual significant physiological changes, also endows
him with important new social capacities. (In primitive societies this period usually marks the entree of the young person
into the adult social life of the group. In our more complex
society the status of childhood is prolonged.) He is now,
biologically at least, a grown-up, and the prospect of adult responsibilities lends a new quality to his educational experience.
This new quality of experience is the imminent fact of responsibility itself. The adolescent or youth no longer lives in a world
which is predominately concerned with his wishes or his demands. The conventions of childhood are no longer adequate
to meet the new requirements which his environment places
upon him. The older child and youth is no longer satisfied
with toys, but wants tools: first toys that will work; then real
instruments that are accountable to the situations in which they
are actually employed, and not merely to an arbitrary world of
his own fancy. There is of course no assumption that the age of
puberty, which varies with individuals, is in itself an exact limit
to "childish" experience as the term here is used. Actually, no
such abrupt demarcation can be made. The change from childhood to responsible adulthood is in all cases gradual. It is also
greatly affected by non-physiological circumstances, including
education itself. But for the purpose of this discussion it may
be assumed that adolescence does, nevertheless, block out
roughly the beginning of a new phase in the pupil's life which
introduces the peculiar problems of secondary education.

If the foregoing analysis is valid it should be clear that secondary education presents distinctive problems not merely be-

cause it deals with pupils who are biologically mature, but also because biological maturity tends to precipitate in education certain aspects of the social problems of the adult community. It is obvious that any further consideration of this problem involves an interpretation of the social function of the school.

The Problem of "Needs"

With respect to the individual, the problem of the social function of the school may be viewed in terms of "needs." The widely discussed question of "needs" concept as a basis of educational planning does not require a detailed review. It must be pointed out, however, that the almost universal recognition of the importance of youth "needs" as a basis for the planning of the Progressive school has not led to convincing results. Public education has been notoriously unsuccessful in meeting fundamental needs of a large proportion of American youth, as pointed out in the foregoing chapter. Whether Progressive schools have been more successful in meeting the problem is, perhaps, less clear.

This raises the question of the definition of "needs" and brings up the familiar problem of the relative weight which should be attached to "psychological" as opposed to "sociological" evidence.

Some Progressive educators have inclined to the view that pupils are the primary source of information regarding their "needs" and that a truly Progressive educator must rely, in large part, upon the "felt needs" and expressed preferences of the pupils themselves.

Others within the Progressive group have opposed this view by emphasizing the point that the needs of youth emerge and find the conditions of their fulfillment or frustration in a social medium which is the fundamental condition of the educational enterprise, in any event. In a recent statement on the subject Bode points out that much confusion has resulted from the too-common assumption that needs can be determined by studying the individual as though he contained the whole answer in himself.[43] Bode suggests that the answers of individual pupils tend to be ambiguous and conflicting because of fundamental inconsistencies in the society. The implication seems to be that if the school has an aim, it is to help individuals resolve the discrepancies and conflicts which impede their normal activities and prevent their growth in a democratic society. Education is in part, at least, an attempt to help people discover what their needs are. The following statement from Bode is illustrative:

It is a commonplace that the infant's only chance to grow into a human being is through social relationships. This is only another way of saying that growth is not directed from within but by the "patterns" embodied in the social order. If we believe in progress in a democratic sense, we must believe that these patterns require continuous revision. As they actually exist in our complex modern world, they not only present conflicting types, but the basic patterns are severally incoherent and internally contradictory. In business, for example, we accept both the profit motive and the ideal of social service; in government we hold to both rugged individualism and the ideal of social security; in the field of esthetics we find that standards are both absolute and relative. Back of all this confusion lies the issue of democracy versus tradition, which must be the central concern of a democratic school.[44]

Quite similar to Bode's position, and perhaps representative of a trend in Progressive thought is the provocative discussion of "needs" in *Reorganizing Secondary Education*.[45] In this discussion Thayer, Zachry, and Kotinsky give explicit attention to the twofold aspects of need as "inner" desire and "outer" lack. The central thesis is that Progressive education must always begin with the expressed preferences of the individual, but that the impulsive leanings of the pupil must always be interpreted with respect to a social environment which lends meaning and direction to what would otherwise be nothing but an explosive

[43] Boyd H. Boyd, *Progressive Education at the Crossroads*, pp. 67 ff. Newson and Company, New York, 1938.

[44] *Ibid.*, p. 71.

[45] V. T. Thayer, Caroline B. Zachry, and Ruth Kotinsky, *Reorganizing Secondary Education*, pp. 25–51. (Report of the Commission on Secondary School Curriculum of the Progressive Education Association.) D. Appleton-Century Company, New York, 1939.

blast of energy.[46] ". . . Desires grow out of past social experience and are formulated in response to confronting social situations, and lacks are always represented in some rudimentary
form in what is longed for." [47] From this discussion one thing,
at least, is clear: To know the individual and to deal with him
intelligently, education must also know the world in which he
lives.

> . . . Education must seek evidence as to the motivations of young
> people, the values of which they are in quest as they go about the
> business of living. Somewhere in this process, too it must seek the
> desirable directions of growth, the types of selfhood better equipped
> to reconstruct social experience so that human quests may be re-
> warded with increasing measures of success.[48]

Whether the foregoing is representative of the trend of thinking among Progressive educators it must be repeated that the
educational implications of such a trend are as yet far from
clear. A question immediately arises whether or not the schools,
and particularly the secondary schools, as presently constituted,
are capable of dealing effectively with the needs of pupils, if
needs are anything more than expressions of impulse and desire.
Closely related is the question of whether or not a Progressive
philosophy of secondary education implies the reconstruction
of its social conditions.

Education and Social Reconstruction

The startling economic dislocations which were disclosed by
the collapse of the stock market in 1929 gave new meaning to
education as a social function. Aroused by the economic crisis
of 1929 and the early 1930's, increasing numbers of teachers
and laymen rallied to the support of a group of educational
leaders whose statements of the early and middle years of the
last decade have now become part of our intellectual tradition.
The writings of Bode, Childs, Dewey, Kilpatrick, Raup, Thayer,
and Hullfish in the *Educational Frontier;* such volumes as those

---

[46] A philosophical treatment of this question is found in: John Dewey, *Human Nature and Conduct.* The Modern Library, New York, 1922.
[47] Thayer, Zachry, and Kotinsky, *op. cit.*, pp. 37–38.
[48] *Ibid.*, p. 39.

of Beard, Curti, Counts, and Newlon in the *Report of the Commission on the Social Studies;* Rugg's *American Life and the
School Curriculum;* the Third Yearbook of the John Dewey
Society, *Democracy and the Curriculum;* the Thirteenth Yearbook of the National Education Association: all these and many
others presented a new challenge to American society and education.

This challenge was based upon the primary fact of cultural
stress in a period of rapid economic and social transition. It was
affirmed that fundamental difficulties in the American society
were due to the retention of an individualistic and uncoordinated form of control in a period of corporate industrialism. In
an age of potential abundance the great technological forces of
modern science were blocked by the profit motive and the waste
of a competitive economy. The "liberties" of private ownership
and control of the instruments of production had become the
fetters of a large proportion of the population, a cause of unemployment and destitution.

The claim that laissez-faire capitalism was primarily responsible for the tremendous gain in our national wealth since the
advent of the machine age was denied. Uncontrolled and unplanned private initiative was identified as a secondary cause of
wealth which had served its day and had now become an obstacle
to social progress. It was asserted that the forces of science,
technology, and human labor were the primary sources of
wealth, and that these great forces should be released through
cooperation.

A new form of society was envisioned as the road to a democracy soundly based on an economy of abundance which would
provide security for all.[49]

The fundamental problem of "social reconstruction" was advanced by educators who saw in the situation the collapse of
outmoded forms of political and economic control, and in edu-

---

[49] This view of the socio-economic crisis was held with some minor variations
in different quarters. It will be recognized as at least roughly characteristic of
the *Educational Frontier* position, and also that of the "experimentalist" group
in education. The economic interpretation was of course shared with many
outside of the educational profession.

cation an important responsibility to join with other social agencies in an effort to save democracy by critical appraisal and reorganization of its economic and industrial processes.[50] The social problem was considered to be also the problem of the schools.

The views of at least many Progressive educators were, by and large, in accord with the position of those who held that American society was facing a critical transition. Many educators who advocated or recognized the imperatives of social reconstruction were also active in the Progressive movement. Probably many Progressive educators who did not subscribe to the thesis of "social reconstruction" were at least receptive to the view that a critical situation was at hand and that formal education was in some measure accountable for the future of American democracy. But the character of the educational function, as social, and the way in which it should be carried out was a matter of vigorous and prolonged discussion. Two main positions developed.

On the one hand, the secondary school had inherited a "methodological" view of the curriculum based upon a conception of growth which found its expression in the familiar dictum that the function of the school is to teach the pupil "how to think, not what to think."

Opposed to this view were some who took the position that the implications of growth in education must be determined with respect to its peculiar and often highly complex conditions at any given time. With respect to the social function of education they agreed upon the necessity of keeping issues informed and open to discussion, but they also held that it was necessary to take a pragmatic view of the democratic process, which was to recognize that even "open-mindedness" and "method" were accountable to their effects. They insisted that actual neutrality in a ruptured situation was impossible, that civil liberties depended upon conditions other than themselves, and that political equality rested not merely upon universal suffrage and the

[50] This position was expressed by George S. Counts in *Dare the School Build a New Social Order?* The John Day Company, New York, 1932.

open forum, but also upon the support of organization and economic power which were commensurate to the required effects of the political activity which happened to be involved.

It is with respect to the possible educational implications of these two views that present tendencies in the "Progressive" reorganization of the high school curriculum must now be considered.

The "Core" as the Answer

More specifically, what is the problem with respect to the organization of the high school curriculum? The dominance of the "core" pattern in Progressive curriculum revision in the secondary schools has been noted. How promising is this development? How valid are its main tendencies with respect to the present difficulties of the secondary school?

One of the dominant characteristics of the "core" type of curriculum is the tendency toward a "psychological" or "methodological" organization of the program in which the "external" demands of "organized subject matter" are subordinated to the present "needs" and "interests" of pupils. Such an interpretation of the "core," however, represents only one important tendency in the progressive movement, whereas the "core" has also come to represent the conception of a common framework of social experience which is essential to the development of each individual. The question appears to be not whether we shall have a curriculum based on "individual needs" or on "essential" experiences, but under what conditions can common educative experiences be utilized as a significant and fruitful medium for the satisfaction and enrichment of human needs.

So far as the practical implications of the "methodological" curriculum are concerned the question may be raised whether the distinction between "psychological" and "logical" organization of curriculum materials tends to a polemical opposition of terms which become somewhat artificial when one attempts to discover exactly what they mean in practice. In theory the quest for "psychological organization" of the curriculum sometimes seems to border on the assumption that materials, or items of "raw" subject matter, are to be found in some neutral state, and that the learner somehow creates a fresh new world each time he undertakes a unit of learning. While this is true in a sense, it is also obvious that the learner "creates" the world *in which he lives* and that this is a world which is common to millions of other learners who are bound to discover it in much the same way.

The pupil-centered curriculum is an important psychological conception. But it does not automatically solve all curriculum problems, especially the problem of continuity, or the progressive reorganization of experience. This, however, will be discussed more fully in the following chapter.

From another approach, the tendency toward a "methodological" curriculum raises important questions with regard to the social function of the school. It is at this point that the conception of Progressive education as teaching "how to think" and not "what to think" becomes a matter of controversy. This question has been vigorously discussed under such headings as "indoctrination," "propaganda," "educational neutrality," and the like, over a period of years. The pertinence of the issue with respect to the present high school program should be clearly defined.

Without here raising the much discussed question of "indoctrination," it is probably fair to say that a good deal of confusion, both with regard to "indoctrination," and the broader question of the social function of education, has been caused by the unfortunate notion that the denial of educational neutrality as a tenable position is equivalent to the assumption that the schools should be "used" by professional and possibly other groups to promote a social revolution. Whether any prominent educator ever entertained the idea of so "using" the schools, this writer is unprepared to say. It seems quite clear, however, that so far as the reconstructionist movement in education has been supported by experimentalism, any such conception of the schools as working against or under an established order would be wholly absurd. One of the most prominent tenets of experimentalism and of Progressive education, as well, has been the integral relationship between school and society. It seems much better to say, therefore, that *the problem of reconstruction is the problem of society and also the problem of the school.* A clear statement of this position is that of Dewey and Childs in the *Educational Frontier*:

> An identity, an equation, exists between the urgent social need of the present and that of education. Society, in order to solve its own problems and remedy its own ills, needs to employ science and technology for social instead of merely private ends. This need for a society in which experimental inquiry and planning for social ends are organically contained is also the need for a new education. In one case as in the other, there is supplied a new dynamic in conduct and there is required the cooperative use of intelligence on a social scale in behalf of social values.[51]

Of course the sameness of the problem of society and education should not be taken to dissolve the identity of the school. The possibilities and limits of education as a constructive social force are vividly suggested in the following quotation from Counts:

> . . . If educational thought is to be effective in modifying practice, it must keep close to society. To what extent the school can influence the direction of social evolution is perhaps an open question; but certainly if it is to achieve this result it must articulate with its own age. Moreover, that it can in any fundamental sense create the impulses which drive society onward, is highly improbable. In a word, the school cannot build a Utopia. . . . A school cannot become socially progressive by mere resolve. . . . The founding of a progressive educational movement is as difficult as the founding of a progressive political party, and for much the same reasons. If it is not rooted in some profound social movement or trend, it can be but an instrument of deception. In spite of all the well-intentioned efforts of intellectuals, society stubbornly chooses its own roads to salvation.[52]

To sum up briefly, education shares the problems and conflicts of the larger community. To use Mannheim's suggestive idea, "modern education is a replica on a small scale of the

[51] William H. Kilpatrick (edr.), *The Educational Frontier*, p. 64. D. Appleton-Century Company, New York, 1933.
[52] George S. Counts, *Secondary Education and Industrialism*, pp. 67–68. Harvard University Press, Cambridge, 1929.

conflicting tendencies which rage in society at large." [53] Thus, to say that the schools should adopt a neutral position toward fundamental controversial issues of modern life is to take an attitude of helpless resignation before the problems of education itself.

The problem of Progressive education in the secondary school is precisely that the activity program is confronted by stubborn social conditions which are essentially frustrating to the normal activities of youth. Secondary education is committed to the heroic task of bridging the interval between childhood and adulthood. Progressive schools seek to make the transition on the basis of an activity program, but the primary end of such a program, the satisfactory induction of youth into our complex industrial and democratic society, tends to be thwarted by present institutional arrangements.

With respect to the high school curriculum the implications of such a position are not difficult to determine. So far as the question of social "neutrality" is concerned the schools are not required to identify themselves with partisan groups, even if they could do so, but rather to provide a truly educative environment for the highly controversial issues and partisan forces which have already invaded the schools with the rise of modern industrial democracy. The evidence seems to show that the public schools are actually partisan, and not democratically educative, under present conditions. One might say that the schools have been used (so to speak) to perpetuate an undemocratic and dualistic educational system which is evidenced in the "youth problem" and the continued separation of "vocational" education from the traditional academic and college preparatory program.

As pointed out in the foregoing chapter this separation of educational functions is attributed to conditions of modern industrialism, and particularly to the difficulties of our present economic system.

If the Progressive secondary school is to become a part of a

[53] Karl Mannheim, *Ideology and Utopia*, p. 138. Harcourt, Brace and Company, New York, 1936.

truly unitary and democratic system of public education, it must bring together in a common educational environment the crucial problems and resources which have so vitally affected the development of the American secondary school. To ignore or to evade such a vital responsibility under the name of "neutrality," "pupil planning," "adolescent needs," or on any other basis, is to ignore the most fruitful possible meaning of Progressive education in this present society.

It must be recognized, of course, that the "core" curriculum actually represents a broad tendency to provide experiences of common value to all pupils in the schools. The "core" experiences are required of all, and various plans are utilized to ensure the common significance and value of the "core" activities. No doubt the use of "social functions," "areas of experience," "problem areas," and other "functional" categories represent highly important attempts to establish an activity program representing *common* needs. It is not clear, however, that the use of the new categories, however suggestive, will in itself serve to bring the Progressive secondary school much closer to the realization of its fundamental purposes.

Some significance is seen in the fact that many "core" curricula are still thoroughly infused by the more or less traditional academic subject matters although these may be regenerated and "functionally" related to "problems" or "units" of study. On the other hand, it is not clear that schools which have attempted to establish an "adolescent needs" program without reference to subject fields or plans of "scope and sequence" have actually succeeded in basing their program on the normal activities (or needs) of youth. If the "core" is to represent activities of common significance and worth it would seem that all American youth should have opportunities to follow their interests and improve their abilities in a common educational setting. Moreover, it would appear that the educative activities of youth should be carried over into the industrial and economic setting which is in some respects the very center of the educational problem. The understandings and attitudes of American youth must be allowed to mature in a democratic educational setting along with their gradual induction into society through actual participation in the occupational activities of the community. Otherwise the "core" will very likely remain a symbol for a regenerated academic curriculum pledged to an activity program, but actually divided from society and unable to provide common opportunities for educative participation and growth in the normal occupational activities of the community.

CHAPTER III
THE CASE FOR A SUBJECT CURRICULUM

In the foregoing chapter certain prevalent conceptions of the activity curriculum were discussed in relation to the Progressive movement in American education, and with particular reference to the secondary school. It was noted how the Progressive reaction was directed against the repression of the spontaneous activities of the young and the imposition of materials and fixed goals. It was also indicated how the Progressive theory and practice were opposed to the traditional school in which pupils were the inhabitants of an artificial world of knowledge-for-its-own-sake and the advancement of individuals along a competitive path to "promotion."

Certain contradictory views and possible confusions and shortcomings in Progressive theory were also advanced. In conclusion it was stated that Progressive views in secondary education have not been sufficiently clarified. It was questioned whether or not some proponents of the activity curriculum had taken sufficient account of the implications of the principles of growth in conjunction with the social function of education as underlying the Progressive secondary school.

In view of the foregoing analysis, the persistence of the traditional curriculum, and the evidences of confusion, failure, and lack of unity in secondary education, the following question is raised: In what respects, if any, do the proponents of the subject-type curriculum represent valid alternatives to the Progressive movement? The question may well be raised whether the confusions, failures, and lack of unity in secondary education may not in some measure be attributed to deficiencies in the growing Progressive movement itself. This problem should be considered from several standpoints. What is the psychology of the "subject" curriculum? What are the possible implications of the social philosophy underlying the "subject" school? And what are the possible positive implications of the case for a "subject curriculum"?

In dealing with the conception of a subject-type curriculum it should be noted, first, that to the writer's knowledge no prominent American educator pretends to support the exact status quo in secondary education, whatever that would be. The arbitrary use of such terms as "conservative" or "reactionary," in connection with the views of those who support a "subject" curriculum, has often tended to obscure issues rather than to clarify them. The existing curriculum, as everyone knows, is one of highly diverse and often conflicting tendencies. Various schools of educational thought react against one another, and also against existing practices and situations in which contrary tendencies work side by side. Most educators are familiar with the wide variations which often exist in practices among classrooms and buildings in the same school system. Some, however, do not appear to see clearly the common problems which confront the Progressive school and that part of the same school which reacts to its Progressive tendencies.

The use of the term "subject curriculum" in this discussion refers, in its minimal sense, to a program of weighted or "essential" learnings which are represented by organized subject matters as opposed to one based primarily on the pupils' "normal," everyday activities. Any other meanings which may belong to the "subject" curriculum will be developed in the ensuing discussion. In general, the case for the "subject" curriculum is directed against two major "misconceptions" or "mistakes" of the Progressive school. The first has to do with an "inadequate" conception of learning as mere adjustment or animal learning, rather than the exercise of distinctly human capacities. The second pertains to the failure to provide a school program based on fundamentally significant subject matters which represent the findings of race experience and the basic arts of civilized man. The following well-known position is selected to illustrate such common meanings of the subject-type curriculum, and also to bring light to bear upon certain possible strengths, and weaknesses, and possible misconceptions in Progressive theory and practice.

The "Essentialist's" Case for the "Subject" Curriculum

In a statement of the "essentialist's" position in 1938 Bagley found that American education was in the grip of theories which were "essentially enfeebling." Under the demands of a constantly expanding school population educators had yielded to the rationalization of the philosophy of "interest" and "pupil freedom" which enabled them to lower standards and thus more easily accommodate the mass education movement. It was this new and "enfeebling" philosophy of education, Bagley stated, which led to the "abandonment of rigorous standards of scholastic achievement," the "disparagement of system and sequence in learning," the "activity movement," the "discrediting of the exact and exacting studies," and the "contrasting emphasis upon the 'social studies'," the "using of the lower schools to establish a new social order," and to the " 'curriculum revision' movement and its vagaries." [1] In Bagley's opinion all these ideas were particularly unfortunate in view of the critical period in which they developed.

Faced with an economic problem without precedent in history, our very way of life was threatened by the political dislocations which were likely to result from the emergence of a new economic and social order, and this danger was intensified by the presence of totalitarian enemies who were watching for signs of weakness. Looking to this threat, Bagley asserted that, "Democratic societies cannot survive either competition or conflict with totalitarian states unless there is a democratic discipline that will give strength and solidarity to the democratic purpose and ideal." [2]

Having made his point for social "discipline" (or "solidarity"), Bagley observed that "American education theory had

[1] William C. Bagley, "An Essentialist's Platform for the Advancement of American Education," *Educational Administration and Supervision*, Vol. 24, pp. 241–256, April, 1938.
[2] *Ibid.*, p. 251.

long since dropped the term . . . from its vocabulary." [3] "To-day," American educators ". . . enthrone the right of even the immature learner to choose what he shall learn. They condemn as 'authoritarian' all learning tasks that are imposed by the teacher. They deny any value in systematic and sequential mastery of the lessons that the race has learned at so great a cost . . ." Thus some educators insist, Bagley declared, upon "the freedom of the learner even when it means that he may later sacrifice the more important freedom from want, fear, fraud, superstition, and error." [4]

Basing their program upon a limited conception of learning which failed to give adequate attention to emergent levels of mental functioning,[5] Bagley found there were many in American education who were ready to discredit systematic learning, and to disregard the essential learnings of the race. There are certain essentials upon which the life of democracy literally depends, and education cannot afford to leave these basic learnings to the individual whim or caprice of the learner, or the teacher. Democracy demands a "community of culture" and this means that each generation must be placed "in possession of a common core of ideas, meanings, understandings, and ideals representing the most precious elements of the human heritage." As to the essentials of the curriculum, "It is by no means a mere accident that the arts of recording, computing, and measuring have been among the first concerns of organized education. They are basic social arts. Every civilized society has been founded upon these arts, and when these arts have been lost, civilization has invariably and inevitably collapsed." [6] To these "basic social arts" Bagley adds a number of other elements, including geography, history, science, the arts, and health instruction. It should also be noted that he tends to favor the separation of special vocational training from the "general education"

[3] *Ibid.*, p. 251.
[4] *Ibid.*, p. 251.
[5] William C. Bagley, *Education and Emergent Man*, Chap. IV. Thomas Nelson and Sons, New York, 1934.
[6] William C. Bagley, "An Essentialist's Platform for the Advancement of American Education," *Educational Administration and Supervision*, Vol. 24, p. 252, April, 1938.

program.[7] The implications of this view, however, will be discussed in the following chapter.

Bagley's conception of the function of education is suggested in the introductory comments already given. The school is to preserve the "basic social arts," to instruct the individual in the essential learnings of the race, and to ensure a "community of culture" based upon common meanings and values. Two elements in Bagley's position require closer examination: first, his conception of learning as pertaining to knowledge and subject matter; and second, his conception of the social function of the school.

Human Learning

For many years Bagley has been one of the outstanding proponents of a curriculum based on "organized subject matter." [8] From the standpoint of his theory of learning Bagley has persistently pointed out that education is a peculiarly human function based upon the distinctively human "ability to accumulate, refine, and transmit learnings." [9] Following his theory of "emergent evolution" Bagley finds that man is biologically continuous with the lower organisms, but that human learning can be understood only on the basis of "emergent functions which are not to be explained in terms of the simpler elements from which they are combined." [10] Human learnings begin on a primitive level which involves the relatively simple stimulus-response situations by which "simple habits" and "specific meanings" are acquired, but as the person matures his learning takes on the emergent, and distinctively human qualities which make possible the acquisition of complex skills and conceptual meanings. This learning at the "conceptual level" is quite different from primitive learning, and is in some respects subject to entirely different laws.[11]

[7] William C. Bagley, *Education and Emergent Man,* pp. 50–51. Thomas Nelson and Sons, New York, 1934.

[8] William C. Bagley, "Is Subject Matter Obsolete?" *Educational Administration and Supervision,* Vol. 21, pp. 401–412, September, 1935.

[9] William C. Bagley, *Education and Emergent Man,* p. 30. Thomas Nelson and Sons, New York, 1934.

[10] *Ibid.,* p. 55.   [11] *Ibid.,* pp. 61–62.

From the standpoint of the distinctively human character of learning, a vital function of education is to aid the individual in the cultivation of "higher mental processes" which involve comprehensive and abstract meanings. Specific meanings are important in learning, but to assume that education can and should be reduced to a series of meanings which are "functional" in the sense that they are required for immediate use, or can be identified with, or reduced to concrete objects, is to oversimplify the educative process. On the emergent levels of learning, in Bagley's view, it is a serious mistake to suppose that education can hold to an "animalistic" theory of human behavior and still accomplish its peculiarly human functions. Hence, to continue with Bagley's argument, there is an important place in education for the systematic and sequential mastery of racial learnings. The organized subject matters of the curriculum are, as Bagley might put it, the necessary counterpart of an "emergent" and "conceptual" level of human learning. For it is by virtue of the accumulated and refined meanings of the race, and also by virtue of man's ability to transmit his experience by symbols, that education derives its most fundamental meanings. Knowledge, to put it another way, is required as "background" and not merely as the "instrumental" solution to an immediate problem. To assume that knowledge is to be learned only when it is needed and immediately applied is to take a narrow and "utilitarian" view which if consistently carried out would tend to a "parsimonious," if not dangerously neglectful, kind of education.[12] The rich learnings of racial experience are tried and proved. Hence, the tendency to deny that there are *essential* subject matters, and the corresponding attempt to base the educational program on a series of incidental or "instrumental" learnings arising out of the impulsions of the young must be regarded as a dissipation of the fundamental intellectual resources of the life of civilized man.

Bagley's conception of the higher levels of human learning, however, does not apply merely to the intellectual aspects of human behavior. If human learning takes on emergent quali-

[12] *Ibid.*, Chap. V.

ties at the "conceptual" level, a similar transmutation may be said to occur with respect to "the volitional side of experience." [13] Thus it is that the mature individual learns to exercise persistent effort toward remote goals, and regulate his conduct on the basis of factors which are qualitatively different from the pleasure-pain motivations of the primitive level of behavior. Bagley therefore questions the widely prevalent notions regarding "interest" and "personal preference" as dominant factors in education. As with respect to the cultivation of the "higher mental processes," Bagley concedes a good deal of weight to the conceptions of "interest" and "spontaneous activities" at the earliest levels of education. His concern is that a "limited" conception of human learning should not impede the intellectual and "volitional" development of the more mature pupil.

The Social Function of Education

Bagley's view of the social function of education is, of course, closely related to his conceptions of human learning, "subject matter," and "volitional maturity." Two of the major functions of the school, as social, have already been indicated: to maintain the basic arts of civilization, and to provide a "community of culture"—a social medium of meanings and values held in common. Somewhat more distinctively characteristic of Bagley's position, however, is his conception of the school as a conservative and stabilizing force in periods of transition. The following quotation is illustrative:

> Paradoxical as it may seem, it is the conservative functions of education that are most significant in a period of profound change. Of the conservation of well established fact and principle there can be no reasonable question, but the sum total of this knowledge (if all departments of human enquiry are included and if hypotheses generally agreed upon by competent scholars as reasonably true and worthy of provisional acceptance as guides to conduct are also included) is literally staggering in its dimensions as compared with the learning capacity of even gifted individuals.[14]

Bagley goes on to say that in eras of rapid change education has a "stabilizing function."

[13] *Ibid.,* pp. 62 ff.
[14] *Ibid.,* p. 154.

. . . The very time to avoid chaos in the schools is when something akin to chaos characterizes the social environment. The very time to emphasize in the schools the values that are relatively certain and stable is when the social environment is full of uncertainty and when standards are crumbling. In the Golden Decade, which ended with the financial crash of 1929, American education, instead of being a stabilizing force, persisted in following the *Zeitgeist*. It seems always to be thus; education follows, it does not lead. . . .[15]

Bagley's conception of educational leadership as involving the reassertation of those values which are "relatively certain and stable" deserves further consideration. The "relatively certain and stable" values would appear to be those which have been established by long, past experience. Once gained, this precious heritage of the past seems to be set off in a higher realm of moral judgments as opposed to the changing and uncertain world of present affairs.

An "Emergent" Realm of Moral Judgments

To illustrate his conception of the status of "moral" values Bagley utilizes his theory of an emergent level of mental functioning in which he finds "a place for the unfettered operation of ideals . . . the plane of moral judgment." On this level, he argues that "conscience" and "free will" may be explained on a "rational basis," that moral behavior may be freed from a "mechanistic interpretation," and that man may once again proclaim a sphere of idealistic conduct which is wholly consistent with modern naturalism, although not continuous with the "lower-order functions" of the human organism. In this sphere [16] a man may truly say that, "I do this because it is right, and for no other reason."

Thus, it appears that the principle of "emergence" in Bagley's theory of "emergent evolution" is employed to establish the priority of racial experience and the dominance of abstract "moral" qualities which are set off from the immediate and pressing affairs of the moment. The role of education is to take

[15] *Ibid.*, p. 155.
[16] William C. Bagley, *Education, Crime, and Social Progress*, pp. 121–123. The Macmillan Company, New York, 1932.

the "long view." [17]   New configurations of social forces cannot be predicted very far in advance. Hence, ". . . organized education on the elementary and secondary levels should be concerned chiefly with those learnings the need for which has persisted in a degree which justifies designating them as 'enduring values in a world of change.' These learnings form the background of social evolution." [18] The racial learnings and "enduring values" came out of the common bedrock of human living, but the fact of their long survival in a world of change gives them a status which is above immediate experience, or the experience of the individual, in much the same sense that human behavior takes on new, emergent qualities at the level of the rational [19] and the moral.[20]

It does not appear that Bagley intends to employ the principle of "emergence," or the sheer fact of survival, as the implicit sanction of established values and existing institutions. The fact of "wholesome and much-needed reform," for instance, is recognized with respect to secondary education.[21] But it is also significant that reforms in education are discussed in connection with "utilitarian values," such as specific occupational training, whereas there are other aspects of the curriculum which represent values of a different kind.[22] Bagley conceives of the development of "ideals" as the "chief work of education," and "ideals" are conceived as different in function from normal "habits" to which they are regulative. Here, again, one finds no evidence of sheer reactionism, as such. A fundamental difficulty, however, remains: If education is to set up inclusive meanings and regulative norms for human behavior, how are such meanings and norms to be determined?

Further clues to Bagley's conceptions of authority and values

[17] William C. Bagley, *Education and Emergent Man*, Chap. XIV. Thomas Nelson and Sons, New York, 1934.
[18] *Ibid.*, pp. 210–211.
[19] *Ibid.*, p. 5.
[20] William C. Bagley, *Education, Crime, and Social Progress*, pp. 121–123. The Macmillan Company, New York, 1932.
[21] William C. Bagley, *The Educative Process*, p. 229. The Macmillan Company, New York, 1916.
[22] *Ibid.*, Chap. XV.

in human affairs are provided in his studies of crime in relation to education.[23] For instance, Bagley stresses "ingrained respect for law" as an important factor in the solution of the problem of criminal behavior. Interestingly, he denies the critical charge that this would indicate that he expects "rejected traditional sanctions to be brought back into force," [24] or that he adheres to "an elaborate, closed, perfected scheme for directing all human behavior." [25] He seems, in fact, to reject any attempt to translate his abstract conception of "respect for law" into social terms, other than something equally abstract, such as "respect for the lives . . . and the rights of others." [26] When he discusses Lippmann's observation that laws become dead when changing conditions take away their value, his reaction is that while this may be true he fails to see how it makes "any less desirable a fundamental predisposition to observe law as such." [27] The indication, apparently, is that Bagley's conception of the control of criminal behavior, if not completely opaque to a cultural interpretation, is at least oddly dualistic in character. This impression is confirmed when he considers Scholtz's conception [28] of the "morally mature man who decides moral questions by weighing the evidence and considering the ends to be attained rather than by emulating the "moralist" and "following the rules." Bagley's significant answer is that he would shun the man who decided moral questions by weighing the evidence—that he would prefer to deal with "a man, even less intelligent, who 'followed the rules.' " [29] The implication, in short, seems to be that Bagley is unable, or unwilling, to translate his conceptions of human values, morality, "discipline," and the like, into their cultural equivalents, and that he prefers to deal with moral problems on the basis of judgments which tend to elevate tradition and es-

---

[23] William C. Bagley, *Education, Crime, and Social Progress,* especially the first three chapters.
[24] *Ibid.,* p. 42.
[25] *Ibid.*
[26] *Ibid.,* pp. 52–53.
[27] *Ibid.,* p. 53.
[28] *Ibid.,* p. 59.
[29] *Ibid.,* p. 59.

tablished "rules," even at the possible expense of their present meaning and effect in human behavior.

It has been noted how Bagley seeks to establish a realm of "social-moral" behavior in which emergent "higher-order functions" (those which represent rational and moral conduct) are presented as the guarantee of moral responsibility. In a certain kind of naturalism Bagley finds a threat to free moral choice and to human "nobility" which he attempts to rescue without involving himself "in treacherous dualisms." The result of this effort is the assertion that human conduct is governed by laws which "transcend" the "lower-order functions." As Bagley puts it, people can act on "simple and immediate" judgments of right and wrong [30] and this statement, which carries a certain psychological validity, becomes the distortion of Bagley's naturalism because he steadfastly refuses, or fails, to give it a social context. To put it in another way, the distinction between "higher-" and "lower-order functions" fails to have clear meaning because the "emergent" levels of human behavior are never given any meaningful content beyond the abstract qualities of "social-moral" behavior. Bagley requests education to accept the "essential" content of "racial experience" without ever making it clear, to the writer at least, how the essential content is to be determined. Hence, the level of "rational" and "moral" conduct is largely stripped of explicit meaning, whereas a somewhat back-broken naturalism is retained by virtue of the racial experience and the "long-time view" which are substituted for the emergent content of present affairs.

It is a rather odd commentary that Bagley's case for a "subject" curriculum should be criticized on the grounds that it fails to take adequate account of the present explicit, and emergent *content* of human affairs. And yet this would seem to be the charge. There appear to be highly suggestive meanings in Bagley's argument for emergent human capacities which are exercised in a social context of established meanings and values, but it would seem to be a one-sided conception of evolutionary man and society which failed to make explicit a deliberate and

[30] *Ibid.*, pp. 121–123.

intelligent method of dealing with emergent conditions and present mutations in human behavior. Thus, from the writer's point of view, the major weaknesses in Bagley's case for a "subject" curriculum is not that he makes a case for essential content in education, and not primarily that he favors an adult-planned curriculum, but rather that the ultimate method by which the content of the curriculum is to be determined is not made clear.

The educational planner is left to choose, so to speak, between the reactionary voice of uncriticized tradition, on the one hand, and an often confused world of competing value systems (all having their roots in "race experience") on the other. Some further implications of this difficulty will be discussed in the following chapter.

Some Positive Implications of the Case for a "Subject" Curriculum

There are, as already suggested, a number of challenging conceptions in the case for the "subject" curriculum. The positive implications of the "subject matter" approach, however, need not be identified necessarily with Bagley's position, nor with the views of other American educators who tend to share Bagley's conceptions of the school curriculum.[31] The "subject" curriculum is probably most accurately viewed as a *tendency* in American education. Moreover, as indicated in the foregoing chapter, there are few, if any, "Progressive" high schools which have totally abandoned courses of "organized" subject matter. In the case of schools which have a "core" curriculum the almost universal tendency is to provide special "subject" courses outside the "core" program itself. It has also been noted, however, that there are some educators who incline to the view that the high school curriculum should go much farther toward the elimination of "subjects" as a basis for the organization of school activities. The possible implications of this conception must therefore be considered with some care. What is the place of

---

[31] Justman groups Bagley with Judd and Morrison as representing the view of "Social Evolutionism" in present theories of secondary education.

Joseph Justman, *Theories of Secondary Education in the United States.* Bureau of Publications, Teachers College, Columbia University, New York, 1940.

"organized subject matter" in the present American secondary school?

The maining of "subject matter," to begin with, is a matter of considerable confusion in discussions of the school curriculum. It has been noted how Bagley defends "systematic and sequential" learnings, "background knowledge," and "subject matter" organized on the basis of "intrinsic relations," as opposed to a narrow "utilitarianism" in educational theory which tends to discredit the "subject," as such.

On the other hand, proponents of a curriculum not based on "subjects" generally degrade prescribed materials in favor of the inclinations of the learner, qualified, of course, by some form of guidance. Pupil purposes become a strategic factor in the selection and organization of learning activities which tend to utilize an increased range of experiences, including some or all of the "logically organized" materials which formerly dominated the entire learning situation. The way in which the individual pupil develops the learning situation under these conditions is sometimes called "psychological organization" in contrast to the imposed "logical organization" of the "subject" curriculum. At this point the controversy often tends to assume an "either-or" form in which "subjects" are opposed to "experience," and "logical" becomes the opposite of "psychological." The obvious fallacies in this statement of the issue have been pointed out. Some educators, on the other hand, have asserted that "subject matter" and "experience" are practically synonymous. "Logical" and "psychological" have been presented as aspects of a single process—matters distinct, perhaps, but certainly not opposed. The lack of a common understanding of these terms, however, continues to be a source of confusion in discussion of the curriculum. It is important, therefore, that these words be given a definite reference.

"Subject matter" has been defined by John Dewey as "the facts observed, recalled, read, and talked about, and the ideas suggested in the course of a development of a situation having a purpose." [32] This includes, but is obviously not identical with, the materials of instruction, insofar as we think of these as printed matter, visual aids, etc. Dewey's discussion in *Democracy and Education* shows the gradual evolution of subject matter from what persons do and say in the primitive community, through the stage of myth and ritual, to the extreme formalization of the accumulated meanings of group experience in modern society.

As the social group grows more complex, involving a greater number of acquired skills which are dependent, either in fact or in the belief of the group, upon standard ideas deposited from past experience, the content of social life gets more definitely formulated for the purposes of instruction . . . probably the chief motive for consciously dwelling upon the group life, extracting meanings which are regarded as most important and systematizing them in a coherent arrangement, is just the need of instructing the young so as to perpetuate group life. Once started on this road of selection, formulation, and organization, no definite limit exists. The invention of writing and of printing gives the operation an immense impetus. Finally, the bonds which connect the subject-matter of school study with the habits and ideals of the social group are disguised and covered up. The ties are so loosened that it often appears as if there were none; as if subject-matter existed simply as knowledge on its own independent behoof, and as if study were the mere act of mastering it for its own sake, irrespective of any social values.[33]

One might say that a good deal of the Progressive reaction in education could be explained as a rediscovery of the ties which bind the school activities to their source in the ideals and ways of living of the social group. Whether the emphasis is placed primarily upon individual development, per se, or upon the improvement of social conditions for individual security and growth, the idea of a "pupil-centered" curriculum is essentially an appeal to experience as the fountainhead and ultimate validation of subject matter. The idea of the "experience curriculum" is still comparatively fresh and therefore tends to invest the terms "subject" and sometimes "subject matter" with the limitations of the educational practices associated with the so-called "subject" curriculum. However, any curriculum, by any name, must necessarily consist of what people do, say, read, and

[32] John Dewey, *Democracy and Education*, p. 212. The Macmillan Company, New York, 1916.
[33] *Ibid.*, p. 213.

observe in the course of their educational experiences; and this, precisely, is subject matter in its full sense. Subject matter consists of the data of experience. Experience, in this sense, is the context of human purposes, methods, and activities in which data acquire meaning. It is therefore absurd to oppose "subject matter" and "experience" as conflicting principles.

It is possible, of course, to make a distinction between "subjects" and "subject matter." The latter term may be employed in a more inclusive sense, whereas the former suggests a system or prescribed sequence of materials in which the "subject matter" has been arranged *for* the pupil. However, the pupil must always deal with systems of materials, in the sense that his behavior necessarily has a social context which includes purposes, meanings, and patterns of behavior other than his own. Items of "subject matter" are not incorporated in experience in the same sense that blocks are arranged in various patterns by a child, but rather come to the learner with their own intrinsic meanings and demands. (In this sense, at least, Bagley's insistence upon the organization of "subject matter" in terms of its own intrinsic relations is valid and suggestive.) This, however, does not mean that the learner does not exercise counter-demands upon the object which takes on new meaning in the learner's experience. To cite a simple example, a youth learns to operate a machine by taking into account the peculiar "principles" of the machine, and behaving accordingly, but he may also, in time, learn to improve the machine, make a better one, or adapt it to better purposes.

The Problem of Continuity

All learning necessarily begins within the experience of the learner, and in this sense it is true that the idea of the pupil-centered curriculum, properly understood, is not a controversial issue, but a psychological fact. Learning starts within the experience of the learner because of the nature of the learning act, not because of educational reforms. But this insight into the learning process, important as it is, will not automatically solve all our curriculum problems. It is widely recognized that

conventional school courses often begin with facts and principles which are beyond the range of experience of the learner.[34]
Large groups in education are now committed to the so-called
"experience" approach. But this is only a beginning. As Dewey
puts it,

> . . . Finding the material for learning within experience is only
> the first step. The next step is the progressive development of what
> is already experienced into a fuller and richer and also more or-
> ganized form, a form that gradually approximates that in which
> subject-matter is presented to the skilled, mature person. . . .[35]

Dewey's main concern, as he goes on to say, is for this second
step, the enrichment of experience and the progressive development of its organization—not that this is less important than
the first step, but because it has received relatively little attention.

The meaning of subject matter in the high school curriculum
must obviously be related to the progressive stages by which the
immature individual is gradually inducted into inclusive social
activities which involve a relatively high degree of organization
and the use of symbols and relatively fixed meanings to ensure
continuity in group behavior. There is no reason to assume that
the activity principle, or the conception of the "experience curriculum," precludes systematic learning when such learning is
meaningful to the maturing pupil.

A question could be raised at this point regarding the meaning of the "core" curriculum as related to the "subjects."
Bagley's conception of the "community of culture" is suggestive
in this connection. And it may be noted in passing that the
"core" has quite consistently recognized "areas" of experience
which are considered essential to all pupils. Further discussion
of this question, however, must be reserved for the following
chapter.

The Progressive school has accepted the "educative experi-

---

[34] This is not in contradiction to the foregoing statement that learning necessarily starts within the experience of the learner. The course which is "above
the pupil's head" or aside from his interest will still be met by the pupil on his
own terms. He will learn *something*, if only to dislike the subject, or the teacher.

[35] John Dewey, *Experience and Education*, p. 87. The Macmillan Company,
New York, 1938.

ence" or the "complete (purposive) act of learning" as the organizing principle of the new curriculum. This being the case it is important that the Progressive school should also take full account of its present social context. Cultural anthropology has contributed much to current educational theory and criticism. Undoubtedly, the study of life in primitive social groups has done much to re-establish a conception of the intimate connections of knowledge and common daily living to the improvement of education. It is not strange, therefore, that enthusiasts should have been tempted to reduce the curriculum to the highly informal pattern of education in the primitive tribe where learning is based almost entirely on direct experience and overt, physical adjustments. In our modern school this type of education no doubt still holds good for the very young. For the learner of increasing maturity contemporary society holds out a vast and complex world of objects, people, and ideas. Today, education functions in a world which has seen the invention of printing and the development of modern science. The experience curriculum obviously cannot ignore the experience of the race.

The conditions of the subject matter of the curriculum are both psychological and social. Educational experiences must adequately reflect the impulses of the learner, but impulses originate and take form in a social medium which gives meaning to human behavior. Subject matter is the raw, inchoate material of growth, but it is also form and direction. Under certain conditions it may be a fostering or retarding influence upon purpose, but it is the structure of purpose as well. The distinctive meaning of the new "psychological" interpretation of the curriculum is not merely that learning is experiencing, but that significant learning experiences always involve the unique perspectives and predilections of the individual; while the truth of the "logical" interpretation of the curriculum is not that learning is passively accepting subject matter, but that the educative experience always involves the learner in a social heritage and group life whose operating purposes, understandings, and techniques provide the conditions and possibilities within which his learning and growth are carried on. The "logical organization" of subject matter may constitute an impediment to learning in much the same sense that rigid institutional frameworks sometimes weigh on the task of intelligent revision in human affairs. But it is equally true that we necessarily operate in and through a given system of postulates, beliefs, and institutionalized practices, whether the enterprise be political or educational.

CHAPTER IV

INTELLECTUALISM AND THE
SOCIAL STRUCTURE OF
THE CURRICULUM

In the preceding chapter the case for a "subject" curriculum, as advanced by one of its outstanding proponents, was examined with respect to certain difficulties, particularly regarding the method by which the "essential" content of such a curriculum might be determined. Some positive implications of the "subject matter" point of view were also developed on the basis of a possible pragmatic interpretation. It was proposed that within its present limits the high school curriculum does, and should, provide for the progressive development of the experience of individuals through systematic learnings representing their gradual induction into responsible participation in the complex and highly organized activities of the community. It was also suggested that the problem of progressive development of experience, or continuity, carries over into the more inclusive meanings and purposes of community activities, as represented by the common essentials of the curriculum, or from a Progressive point of view, the "core." Finally, it was noted that while the "experience" approach to curriculum planning represents a significant advance in educational theory, the "educative experience" becomes an adequate guide to the organization of the school program only if considered in integral relation to a social context which provides the fundamental directions and conditions of the educative process. This assumption, growing out of the preceding chapter, should now be considered at length.

As in the foregoing chapter the problem is developed with reference to certain views in the "new education" as seen in relation to an alternative position. The purpose of this chapter is in some respects continuous with that of the preceding one:

namely, to bring into perspective some possible weaknesses in Progressive views of the high school curriculum. In this case, another challenging position is studied to throw light on the problem of setting up fundamental aims for the secondary school program. Particular attention is given to the method of defining fundamental educational purposes, and its main implications with regard to the curriculum. (A preliminary question might be raised as to whether the philosophy of Progressive education permits the conception of dominant educational purposes except as such aims evolve out of the daily purposive activities of pupils.) [1]

Those who have followed the curriculum "revision" movement in recent years no doubt have been impressed by the frequency of the word "tentative," as used in describing courses of study. Sometimes the impression is given that the most prominent characteristic of the "curriculum planner" is his persistent inability, or refusal, to make up his mind. It should be added at once, of course, that the practice of re-examining fixed courses of study, handed down from one year, and even from one generation to the next, is an utterly wholesome one. The question to be raised is not regarding the values of flexibility and openness to changing conditions, but whether or not "tentativeness" carried beyond a certain point may not be a signal of weakness in an educational position. Some educators would say that the problem is whether or not an educational program can go on indefinitely without deciding what it is educating for. Briggs, for instance, has long pointed to the evidences of confusion in secondary education, with the challenge that adequate and clear-cut aims must be defined for the schools (and for the American society as well). The meaning of democracy must be clearly defined. Once the society has decided upon its direction it should then be possible for secondary education to make an intelligent and consistent plan.[2]

The problem may well be raised whether a good deal of the

[1] This question is of course closely related to the issues discussed in the conclusion of Chapter II.

[2] Thomas H. Briggs, *Secondary Education*, pp. 114 ff. The Macmillan Company, New York, 1937.

confusion in the present secondary schools, including many which show marked Progressive tendencies, is not due to continued failure to establish fundamental objectives sufficiently comprehensive and significant to comprise the suitable basis of a common school program for American youth.

Hutchins' Proposal for "General Education"

One of the best known criticisms of the aimlessness and confusion of American education is that which has been put forth by President Hutchins of the University of Chicago. Since Hutchins also represents challenging alternatives to some of the main underlying conceptions of the Progressive school, particularly with respect to the question of determining fundamental educational aims, a brief analysis of his position should help to bring the problem of this chapter more clearly into view. It should be noted, however, that his plan for "General Education" is not merely a criticism of the Progressive school, nor of its philosophical assumptions. The critical attack is made on a wider basis, and is directed to various tendencies in American society and education.

Reviewing Hutchins' argument, one is first impressed by his intense concern for the state of confusion in American education. He finds that, "The most striking fact about the 'higher learning' in America is the confusion that besets it. This confusion begins in the high school and continues to the loftiest levels of the university." [3] The high school is unable to make up its mind whether to educate for college or for life. The universities, on the other hand, are beset by many ills which result largely from the fact that educational policies are determined by the people (students, donors, legislatures) whose thinking is dominated by "utilitarian" ideals on the one hand, and by a false conception of democracy in education on the other.

. . . the people love money and think that education is a way of getting it. They think too that democracy means that every child should be permitted to acquire the educational insignia that will be

[3] Robert Maynard Hutchins, *The Higher Learning in America*, p. 1. Yale University Press, New Haven, 1936.

helpful in making money. They do not believe in the cultivation of the intellect for its own sake.[4]

Hutchins' second main criticism of American education is advanced in the charge of "anti-intellectualism." Generally speaking the schools have renounced their primary function, and the vital matter of intellectual development has been sacrificed to specific vocational training or to the mere acquisition of information.[5] The confusion of society which might be resolved by genuine intellectual leadership in education is only fostered by the schools themselves. The situation is especially grave because the causes of confusion in education are basically social: ". . . the state of the nation determines the state of education." On the other hand, the state of the nation can be improved only through education. Hence we are caught in a vicious circle. "The state of the nation depends on the state of education; but the state of education depends on the state of the nation." This vicious circle can be broken upon one condition: that some of our educational institutions "can be strong enough and clear enough to stand firm and show our people what the higher learning is, . . . "(namely)" . . . the single-minded pursuit of the intellectual virtues." [6]

The foregoing argument is, of course, found in the context of a statement on higher education. But Hutchins makes it clear that in his view the problems of "higher learning" are continuous with certain fundamental issues involving the reorganization of the entire educational program from the beginning of the secondary school on. The confusion in "higher learning" (which reflects the confusion of society itself), its "professionalism," the "isolation" of its departments, its "anti-intellectualism"—all stems from one source: failure in communication, the absence of a common fund of ideas.

We can never get a university without general education. Unless students and professors (and particularly professors) have a common

---

[4] *Ibid.*, p. 31.

[5] Robert Maynard Hutchins, "Ideals in Education," *The American Journal of Sociology*, Vol. 43, No. 1, p. 8, July, 1937.

[6] Robert Maynard Hutchins, *The Higher Learning in America*, p. 32. Yale University Press, New Haven, 1936.

intellectual training, a university must remain a series of disparate schools and departments, united by nothing except the fact that they have the same president and board of trustees. Professors cannot talk to one another, not at least about anything important. They cannot hope to understand one another.

We may take for granted that we shall always have specialists; yet neither the world nor our knowledge of it is arbitrarily divided up as universities are. Everybody cannot be a specialist in every field. He must therefore be cut off from every field but his own unless he has the same basic education that other specialists have. This means more than having the same language and the same general interest in advancing knowledge. It means having a common stock of fundamental ideas.[7]

The Functions of General Education

On closer examination, it is apparent that Hutchins has in mind two main educational functions, or perhaps more accurately, a single function with two main aspects. The program of "general education" is recommended for each one, whether he is to go on to the university or not. It is considered to be highly useful, but its usefulness is not practical in the ordinary sense. "It may not assist him to make money or to get ahead. It may not in any obvious fashion adjust him to his environment or fit him for the contemporary scene." What, then, will it do? "It will have a deeper, wider utility; it will cultivate the intellectual virtues."[8] The job of "intellectual training," according to Hutchins, should be the central aim of schools and the particular function of "general education."

But it is more than this; it is an important social goal as well. In fact, it is "the good for which all other goods are only means. Material prosperity, peace and civil order, justice and the moral virtues are means to the cultivation of the intellect."[9] Hutchins begins with the problem of "confusion" in higher education, a confusion which reflects the condition of society itself, and ends with the conclusion that the way out is through that kind of "general education" which links man with man. From the social point of view the problem is one of communication; for

[7] *Ibid.*, p. 59.
[8] *Ibid.*, p. 62.
[9] *Ibid.*, p. 67.

the individual it is the cultivation of the "intellectual virtues." And the means through which these aims are to be realized are found in a program based on the content of "race experience."

The content of Hutchins' program is selected with the foregoing ends in view. On the one side, it consists of the fundamental arts of communication and reason: "grammar," "rhetoric," "logic," and "mathematics;" and on the other the "permanent studies," and particularly the "great books." [10] An education based on such content will do two things: It will teach man how to use his mind and how to communicate. And it will also assure his familiarity with the basic ideas of the race, or at least with those ideas which "can seriously pretend to be basic."

The Philosophy of "General Education"

Without undertaking a detailed analysis of Hutchins' position, certain main elements must briefly be discussed. To begin with, Hutchins' theory is based on an intellectualistic conception of learning which tends to discount the "biological" view of human behavior, and with it, the native preferences and impulsions of the learner. Contemporary psychology, in Hutchins' belief, has failed to give education an adequate view of learning because it is preoccupied with a partial view of human nature. ". . . In so far as psychology deals with anything of importance, it is physiology—all about muscles and the central nervous system. The nature of man as distinguished from the other animals scarcely appears in it. . . ." "The result," Hutchins continues, "is that there is no such thing as the intellectual life of man. The mind is regarded as a biochemical mechanism developed to solve practical problems. . . ." [11]

But the human mind is actually much more. And the true nature of mind is revealed in the character and objects of knowing, which is opposed to merely "knowing how." To know, that is, is not merely to make an immediate and "practical" adjustment to a situation. The mind is an instrument of reason, and

[10] *Ibid.*, esp. pp. 77–87.
[11] Robert Maynard Hutchins, "The Philosophy of Education," in *The William Rainey Harper Memorial Conference*, pp. 40–41. The University of Chicago Press, Chicago, 1937.

as such its function is to strike beneath the changing "conventions" of life to nature, itself, which is fundamentally unchanging. ". . . To the extent that men are rational they have found and will doubtless continue to find that they can and should agree on matters of knowledge, although they may still disagree on matters of opinion. . . ." [12]

Thus, the conception of mind is integrally related to Hutchins' world-view which is diametrically opposed to the notions of contemporary experimentalism. In a statement on "The Philosophy of Education," Hutchins asserts that American education has been led astray by a false empirical "naturalism" which "leads us to concern ourselves not with nature but with experience." He adds that "Empiricism is content with experience," whereas "true naturalism would pass through experience to the nature of things." [13] It is in this view of nature that Hutchins' conception of mind finds its meaning. ". . . Knowledge has nature for its object: the essential, the universal, the uniform. . . ." [14] The function of mind is *to know*, not merely to get information. And by the same token, the function of science, "when it is true science, is not the collection of data; it is the determination of general laws." [15]

The characteristic statement of Hutchins' philosophy of the curriculum is well known. "Education implies teaching. Teaching implies knowledge. Knowledge is truth. The truth is everywhere the same. Hence education should be everywhere the same. . . ." [16]

The fundamental emphasis of Hutchins' argument is upon the need for a body of principles which will order the function of "intellectual" leadership in the schools. The long discussion over the question of the particular metaphysics of his position

---

[12] Robert Maynard Hutchins, "A Reply to Professor Whitehead," *Atlantic Monthly*, Vol. 158, p. 587, November, 1936.

[13] Robert Maynard Hutchins, "The Philosophy of Education," in *The William Rainey Harper Memorial Conference*, p. 35. The University of Chicago Press, Chicago, 1937.

[14] *Ibid.*, p. 37.

[15] *Ibid.*, p. 38.

[16] Robert Maynard Hutchins, *The Higher Learning in America*, p. 66. Yale University Press, New Haven, 1936.

need not be brought up here. Two final observations, however, should be made. There is obviously a striking resemblance between Hutchins' position and the medieval philosophy of Thomistic Aristotelianism, to which he professes a strong affinity. . . . If Hutchins is not attached to a particular set of basic ideas, but only to the conviction that education needs a well-defined aim, then he has left his audience very few (if any) intelligible cues as to how such an aim should be determined. On the one hand, there is the "cultivation of the intellectual virtues," and on the other, the fundamental "experience of the race," as in the "great books." The final conclusion of the argument is not entirely clear, but it would seem to be that there are certain self-evident or a priori "truths" which become clear to those who have had the proper "intellectual" training, and, of course, the native ability to deal with ideas. The findings of experimental science, on the other hand, appear to take a secondary role to the "true" function of science which is based on the recognition of immutable principles as rooted in "human nature" and the world in which we live. The distinctive meaning of the modern conception of experimental science as discovery is thus wiped out because science can only discover what it is bound to find, and what has probably been discovered already, anyway.

The net conclusion, then, is that Hutchins makes a compelling case for educational direction, but that his particular statement of the case leaves one to grapple with vague and elusive, or possibly authoritarian, implications.

Dewey stated his criticism of Hutchins' thesis in a series of articles which appeared in the *Social Frontier* in 1936 and 1937.[17] The center of his attack is Hutchins' conception of "the inherent nature of knowledge and intelligence in relation to matters intellectual."[18] In line with Dewey's argument, the most effective pragmatic answer to intellectualism, so far as education is concerned, is to call into account the methods by which human decisions are related to the peculiar conditions out

[17] Vide *Social Frontier*, Vol. 3, Numbers 21, 22, 24.
[18] John Dewey, "The Higher Learning in America," *Social Frontier*, Vol. 3, No. 24, pp. 167–169, March, 1937.

of which they arise. Intellectualism, or any other brand of educational philosophy which fails to make explicit the grounds upon which judgments are made, or which stands, implicitly or otherwise, for a rigid frame of values aloof from any attempt at experimental verification, must of course answer to Dewey's question.

While the respective positions of Hutchins and Bagley are quite different in many respects, it may be noted that they share a strong inclination to rely upon ordering "values" or "truths" without dealing adequately with the methods by which such principles are to be obtained. Particularly evident, in both cases, is an apparent lack of concern over competing value systems which, in the absence of an experimental method of verification, would seem to make contradictory and perhaps equally strong claims as to the confirmation of "race experience," on the one hand, or "truth," on the other. Granting that some of the "established" values and "eternal verities" may be "true," one is left to ponder how the verification is made so long as experimental science must always be applied within an ordering framework of prior judgments.

Education, Values, and Science

The case for "subjects" as representing the systematic and progressive development of experience has been considered in the preceding chapter. The question may now be raised as to a possible pragmatic interpretation of some of the problems which are suggested by the intellectualistic criticism of Progressive education. One is bound to concede the strength of Hutchins' charge as to confusion in American education. One also recalls his statement that we are living in an intellectual tradition whether we like it or not.[19] Moreover, there is an inspiring challenge in Hutchins' dignified view of educational leadership and clear-sightedness, however unsatisfactory his underlying assumptions may be, from another point of view.

So far as Hutchins, and other exponents of a fixed-content cur-

---

[19] Robert Maynard Hutchins, "Ideals in Education," *American Journal of Sociology*, Vol. 43, No. 1, p. 8, July, 1937.

riculum, are speaking to pragmatic influences in Progressive education it should be noted that pragmatism is not opposed to an ordering of values, as such. As a philosophy, pragmatism has been widely viewed as a method, but the experimentalists themselves have not been unaware of certain basic assumptions, the framework, at least, of a metaphysic.[20] It is equally clear that the pragmatist is well aware that authority resides within the context and movement of human affairs. Man's existence, he would agree, is largely ordered by objective arrangements and institutions. It is obvious, of course, that pragmatism has often tended to a negative form of protest against existing institutional arrangements which are criticized in the light of changing conditions and new social demands, but the positive implications are no less clear. The fact of a changing world is not in contradiction to a conception of human behavior as structured. Indeed, it is the keen perception of "habit" and structure in human affairs which has prompted the experimentalist to give so much attention to its implications in a complex and rapidly changing society.

As Dewey expresses it, ". . . All of the actions of an individual bear the stamp of his community as assuredly as does the language he speaks. Difficulty in reading the stamp is due to variety of impressions in consequence of membership in many groups. . . ." Significantly, he adds, "This social saturation is . . . a matter of fact, not of what should be, not of what is desirable or undesirable." [21]

It is apparent that the experimentalist is fully aware of systems of values which are imbedded in the structure of human behavior. But from the standpoint of his fundamental faith in democracy and the scientific method (which are primary values in pragmatism) he insists that no arrangement of values or "truths" should be permanently removed from the reach of the experimental test and the final judgment of human beings.

If Hutchins stands for a curriculum based on "ultimate" prin-

[20] John L. Childs, *Experimentalism and the Philosophy of Education,* esp. Chap. 3. D. Appleton-Century Company, New York, 1931.
[21] John Dewey, *Human Nature and Conduct,* p. 317. The Modern Library, New York, 1922.

ciples and "eternal" verities which are beyond the reach (or which over-reach) experimental scientific method, then it might be said that Progressive education is generally based on a contrasting faith in the ultimate reliability of science as the only permanently satisfactory basis of human behavior in a changing world of novel events and emergent characters. Such a contrast, however, would be an over-simplification of the case.

It is noteworthy that Progressive education incorporated the tradition of experimental science but that there were other elements which influenced its development, and also, that Progressivism was in some respects a reaction against the "scientific movement" in American education. So far as the theoretical foundations óf the movement were concerned, at least, Progressivism was opposed to the ultra-positivism of the "scientific movement" because it had certain ordering values, including the democratic ideal and the conception of "growth," which could not be reconciled with the utter neutrality of the "social and vocational activity analysis" conception. Thus, the "activity" principle in Progressive education, as viewed in this study, is less than "Progressive" if it is not linked with some conception of the relative educative and social values of different kinds of activities, as well as some idea of the continuous growth of the activity, itself.

It is clear that Progressive education has the framework, at least, of a system of ordering values. It is not clear that the Progressive schools have been in practice much less naively "empirical" than were those which subscribed to the "activity analysis" movement prior to its general decline. In theory modern Progressive educators have rejected the mirror-like function of the school which only perpetuates the present activities of the community. "Adolescent needs," and similar conceptions, have been taken by some as the rejection of a value-less empiricism on the one hand, or the arbitrary imposition of adult views, on the other. Unfortunately, it is still not clear that "adolescent needs" do not often merely reflect adolescent preferences which in turn mirror present activities and established conventions of "growth" in the community. Is it not possible, in other words, that the "needs" approach to educational planning often tends to fall back into the very kind of positivism which under the name of the "scientific movement" was discredited by Progressive educators themselves? Since the discussion of this problem hinges in some fundamental respects on the modern conception of experimental science, it should be useful to consider briefly the case of the sciences at the present time.

The Social Function of Science

One could almost draw a parallel between the retreat from "subjects" in education and the current unrest in the scientific world. Since the Great War the conditions of human knowledge have become more and more an object of investigation. Science has tended to become increasingly self-conscious. Even physics has been obliged to acknowledge the important fact that the observer is a part of the field with respect to which his findings are made.

As to their social function, one is constantly reminded that science and technology operate in concrete social settings which affect not only the immediate ends to which technological instruments are employed, but also the methods by which these instruments are modified and improved. The peculiar effects in science of the Nazi movement, for instance, are noted by Bernal.

. . . It is quite clear that, from the point of view of the philosophy of blood and soil, science is fundamentally unnecessary. But deliberate intellectual barbarism, the conscious repudiation of the European tradition of culture as un-German, is only one side of the Nazi movement. The other, and increasingly predominant side, is the development of German world power. It is in the field of science that these two aspects appear in the most glaring contradiction. It would be very grand if the German youth could defy the world and establish their superiority by their naked strength. Unfortunately, present-day warfare requires machinery and a heavy economic backing, and for these science is necessary. The Nazis are faced with the paradox of having to maintain their strength by the use of methods which they despise. The survival of German science depends on the need which the military and economic state has for its work. There is, however, the greatest confusion as to how much and what kind of science is needed for this purpose. German technique has for years been one of the highest in the world; it is based on science but does not, if it has simply to maintain itself, require any further application of it. On the other hand, if military successes are to be gained and the country made independent of all foreign sources of supply, it is necessary not only to maintain but also to improve and create new technical means, and for this science cannot be dispensed with. It can, however, be sharply limited to the attainment of these ends. There has been, consequently, a deliberate policy of turning science into Wehrwissenshchaft, of encouraging those researches, and those researches only, which tend to direct or indirect military ends. . . .[22]

Most observers make a general distinction between those sciences which have to do with the world of "natural" affairs and those which deal with the "social." In the latter it is customary among some intellectual groups to read cultural bias into most of the materials. Even the relatively "neutral" field of anthropology, for instance, turns out to have a "Nazi" interpretation. It should be added that the absurdity of this particular perversion of anthropology hardly serves to discredit a sociological view of knowledge, but rather emphasizes the fact that scientific behavior has a social matrix which must give direction —which may distort or even destroy the scientific enterprise itself.

It would be superficial and evasive to dismiss the fascist regimentation and suppression of science as merely a perversion— to insist that science, in the sense of "Pure Science," is above human motives save those, perhaps, which represent the quest of "truth for its own sake." Science, like the church, is a human enterprise. There is little to be gained by dividing its effects into two parts and disclaiming responsibility for that which is regrettable. The ideal of "Pure Science," according to Bernal, appears to have some relation to conditions which prevent or pervert the application of scientific methods to matters of human welfare. In the seventeenth century the scientists insisted on the practical utility of their efforts in order to gain needed support. They had every confidence that the extension of their work would be to the benefit of society. By the nineteenth century "it became apparent that science could be, and was being, put to base uses." It was then that the modern

[22] J. D. Bernal, *The Social Function of Science*, pp. 217–218. The Macmillan Company, New York, 1939.

version of the ideal of "pure science—without thought of application or reward" took form.[23]

The typical reaction to the attitude of "pure science" and its effects have been vividly portrayed by Hogben. As he expresses it,

> . . . The exaltation of "pure" thought which bears no fruit in action exacts its own penalty in the growing disposition to regard reason and progress as exploded liberal superstitions. The younger generation have found us out. Their pitiable predilection for action without thought is the legitimate offspring of thought divorced from action.[24]

Bernal points out that because of its close connection with industry, modern science has become an institution. Like other institutions it is "dependent on the existing social order, it is recruited in the main from the same section of the population and it is saturated with the ideas of the dominant classes."[25] It is all too easy, he reflects, to take for granted the continued existence of an institution which developed in pace with the industry of expanding capitalism. No doubt its continued existence and effects will depend in some large degree upon the social context in which its future direction and meaning is to be found. This, of course, does not mean that science merely implements political and economic behavior. It does mean that the preservation of the scientific spirit and the continued progress of the scientific enterprise will depend upon the willingness of scientists and others to recognize and to assume some responsibility for the ends to which techniques and instruments are applied.

For one reason, the problem of modern science is difficult because its methods were first developed in "the study of systems where everything is uniform and nothing really new happens."[26] Bernal points out that the theory of evolution marked an important step not only in our understanding of nature but in our method of thinking as well. It is this new outlook of science

---

[23] *Ibid.*, pp. 95–98.

[24] Lancelot Hogben, *The Retreat from Reason*, pp. 9–10. Watts and Company, London, 1936.

[25] Bernal, *op. cit.*, p. 11.

[26] Bernal, *op. cit.*, p. 413.

which holds out the promise that man will somehow learn to deal rationally with the novel elements in his universe, including the promising and also threatening effects of his own technological genius.

The actual extension of the area of the rational to include what Mannheim calls the "irrational," or the unplanned, will be tedious and slow, possibly too slow. Moreover, in the attempt to control his environment man as scientist will be obliged always to work with existing tools which are not perfect, and within limits which fall short of the Utopian. Scientific method, in other words, must rely upon the conditions which it seeks to transform.

The Social Structure of the Curriculum

The case with the school curriculum is somewhat analogous to that of science in that education works within a social framework which provides the fundamental directions and conditions of the educative enterprise. The "subject," in so far as it reflects the continuity and structure of human activities, is both the condition and the object of learning.

The resolution of this dilemma is not accomplished by simply denying the sociological foundations of the school program. The dangers of the conventional "subject" curriculum are twofold: first, that it may help to perpetuate habits which are no longer well adapted to the changing conditions of human welfare, and second, that it may help to segment or mechanize human activities in such a way that underlying conflicting motives are disguised or obscured. The "experience" curriculum, even though it is usually defined in psychological terms, presents at least the possibility of obviating such dangers.

Its limitations, on the other hand, are denoted by the fact that human resources are developed and utilized within the matrix of existing cultural and political configurations. There is an element of truth, for instance, in Morrison's conception of an *existing* curriculum.[27] The fact of cultural change does not

---

[27] Henry C. Morrison, *The Curriculum and the Common School*, p. 5, also Chap. II. The University of Chicago Press, Chicago, 1940.

efface the institutional framework of society which provides the
conditions and possibilities of growth and creative innovation
at any given time. The concept of the "experience" curriculum
is a real challenge to the school of fixed content and aim. Its development, however, will gain strength and direction to the extent that it is able to take account of the explicit social conditions upon which it rests and to express adequately the most
fundamental and inclusive purposes of its democratic and industrial tradition. What, then, are the main concrete implications with respect to the curriculum of the secondary school?

The "Core" and the Aim of Secondary Education

In the preceding chapter it was suggested that the "core" curriculum represents the continuity of broadly social aspects of
human activities in somewhat the same way that the special
"subjects" or "courses" tend to pertain to the more diversified
activities of the community. Thus, "personal-social problems"
or some form of "general science" may be considered suitable
for all pupils, whereas "aviation mechanics" or college-preparatory physics may be offered as "electives."

On somewhat the same basis, a distinction can be drawn between the subject matter of the "core" curriculum and the
"subjects" of "special" education, in view of the fact that man as
specialist enjoys a certain relative degree of immunity from the
exigencies of social change, whereas his activities in their
broader social and political aspects reflect the changing conditions, problems, and purposes of the society in a much more
direct way. A mechanic, a machine-tool operator, or a physicist
may employ similar knowledges and skills in vastly different
social situations, and for greatly different purposes. Their problems as specialists, and as persons or citizens, are integrally related, of course, but certainly not identical.

In view of these considerations there can be little question
why the "core" curriculum should have made its appearance
in a period marked by profound and disquieting social changes.
In a highly stable and unchanging society there would be little
or no occasion for a "core," or at least the "core" would be

buried in the traditional constants of the curriculum. In a democratic and changing society the case is quite different. Special disciplines may be expected to remain as useful electives for individual purposes. New "subjects" may be expected to appear. At the same time, those aspects of the curriculum which are related to common problems tend to become volatile. It is at this point that the "core" with its reaction against "subject" organization and its "methodological" emphasis tends to emerge. It is recognized, of course, that the actual development of such a program depends upon an appropriate educational philosophy.

The assumption, obviously, is that the "core" curriculum is, in its most profound sense, an attempt to define adequate social (and personal) goals when directions are changing and customary goals are called into account. The critical bearing of Hutchins' proposal for "General Education" may be recalled at this point. Again, his conception of vigorous and clear-sighted leadership must be contrasted with the corresponding tendency in some Progressive schools to rely heavily upon the emerging purposes of the pupils, as developed in school activities, or in their "daily living." Now the argument against the seemingly authoritarian implications of Hutchins' position has been made. In the writer's view there is no reason to assume that an intellectual elite, trained in the universities, should somehow have possession of the "final answers," or that if they did, it would make any material difference in the world "below." If Hutchins questions the ability of the public schools to change society, then it would appear that a similar question might be directed at his assumption that the universities can start a "spiritual revolution" [28] which will cure our social ills.

The question is not whether the schools, or the universities, can lift themselves and society by their own bootstraps, but whether there is any justification in the view that the "core" curriculum can undertake to fulfill its fundamental purposes within the social and intellectual limitations which now dominate the "core" in many schools. Is it probable, one may ask,

[28] Hutchins, *op. cit.*, p. 10.

that "adolescent needs" as expressed by pupils or as defined merely by a local planning group [29] will be likely to give adequate expression to fundamental social problems which are literally nation-wide in scope, or to result in clearly defined purposes representing the most inclusive views of present social and educational problems? One is reminded of Hogben's comment in the *Retreat from Reason*:

> A disturbing omen of cultural decadence is an attitude common among those regarded as educational reformers. To acquire a reputation in this capacity you need only replace the formula, knowledge is an end in itself, by the dogma, childhood is an end in itself. This means that we are to stop thinking about what kind of knowledge an age of potential plenty requires from its citizens and leave the child to decide what it likes best, a policy which conveniently promotes both teacher and pupil to the leisured class. Naturally it is important that some people should study how to make children happy if their happiness is compatible with their happiness in later life, . . . if it is clear that happiness is the concern of psychological medicine and not the primary business of education. The trouble is that so many of our educational reformers do not realize that pediatrics is one thing and pedagogy is another.[30]

The question may well be raised whether the "core" curriculum, or the somewhat broader tendencies and practices of the Progressive high school program, as now widely viewed, have adequately expressed the fundamental democratic purposes of American life and education. This question, of course, is not for Progressive education alone.

What are the social premises of the present American secondary school? Has it taken into completely honest account the American tradition of equality of educational opportunity, and the specific social and economic conditions which now endanger this ideal? Has it provided the conditions of cumulative intellectual and social growth as based on activities which are genu-

[29] "The trend in curriculum construction throughout the country is away from state-wide or city-wide formulations toward individual-school curriculum reorganization." H. H. Giles, S. P. McCutcheon, and A. N. Zechiel, *Exploring the Curriculum, Adventure in American Education*, Vol. 2, p. 22. (Commission on the Relation of School and College, Progressive Education Association.) Harper and Brothers, New York, 1942.

[30] Lancelot Hogben, *Retreat from Reason*, pp. 60–61. Watts and Company, London, 1936.

inely significant and honestly promising in the lives of young people? More specifically, has the secondary school, whether in its Progressive or its more traditional aspects, offered a plausible and possibly effective answer to the needs of millions of American youth who vainly strive for gradual and normal induction into the life of the "adult" community? Has it considered the full implications of the fact of millions of young men and women who in times of peace are unemployed, or whose education is provided in the youth work agencies?

These questions will be considered in the following, and final, chapter.

CHAPTER V

LOOKING TOWARD
A NEW PROGRAM
OF YOUTH EDUCATION

THE American high school grew out of the rich promise of American life. It was based on the vast resources of a virgin continent and its main growth was parallel to the rise of a great industrial system. The social and economic changes that occurred with the industrialization of American life: the growth and urbanization of the population, the rising standard of living, changing patterns of employment and family life as affecting youth—all of these were among the factors which affected the development of our system of free, universal secondary education.

However, the high school was also a fundamental expression of the democratic ideal in American life. In a very real sense its nineteenth and twentieth century development in this country was continuous with the common school movement which first took form with the beginnings of liberalism in the medieval towns of Europe. In this country, as in Europe, there are many indications that the rise of the common school was intimately related to social and intellectual changes which came about with the development of the modern liberal-industrial state. But in the United States the uniquely favorable conditions were such that the common school was extended to include the secondary level. The development of free, universal, and secular education up to and including the secondary school was based on the wealth of its material conditions and possibilities, and the spirit of the American democratic ideal.[1]

But the public high school was not based wholly upon the

---

[1] A detailed account of the rise of the American high school out of its common school origins is given in Chapter I.

promise of an abundant and expanding national life. It also reflected the changing conditions and emerging problems of a society whose prospects were threatened by frustration and the possible collapse of not only its economic life but the democratic ideal itself. The preceding chapters have dealt with the changing character and demands of the expanding high school population; the persistence of the "college-bound" and traditional curriculum in the midst of largely unplanned expansion and sometimes chaotic change; the critical nature of what came to be called during the 1930's the "youth problem"; and the appearance of the youth work agencies with their implicit challenge to the democratic conception of a unitary public school affording equal opportunities for all.

One recalls that the curious ambiguity of the American high school was first evidenced in the fact that its main development was in some large part due to a mounting national wealth and to the growing effects of economic failure [2] and contraction, at the same time. Thus, the secondary school remained a symbol of "success" and the fading promise of employment in "business" or in the "white-collar" professions, even while it became more and more a vast reservoir for youth who were barred from gainful employment by changing technical and economic conditions. After 1929 the discrepancies of American society and education became startlingly clear. The free public high school had scored a great success in terms of its unparalleled growth, but it had also dismally failed. The unitary public school system was based upon American democracy and the promise of an abundant life for all the people. The educational dimensions of the prospects of this society were summed up in the conception of equal educational opportunities for all the children of all the people. The threatened failure of this conception could not, and cannot, be divorced from the social conditions upon which it rests.

[2] "Failure" is used in the sense of inability to use available human and material resources in the presence of unemployment and poverty.

Progressive Education Offers an Alternative
to the Traditional School

From the standpoint of the high school curriculum one important aspect of the problem of secondary education was brought into focus by the Progressive challenge to the traditional high school program. This challenge of the Progressive movement was directed against the curriculum of traditional and fixed "subjects" as representing college-entrance requirements and conventional adult conceptions of pupil needs. Basing their attack upon the initial observation that the "college preparatory" curriculum was obviously not adapted to the needs of a large proportion of American youth, Progressive educators sought to apply in the secondary school vital new conceptions which were already widely employed in elementary education.

Perhaps the primary idea underlying the Progressive movement was that *the daily living activities of the individual are educative.* From the standpoint of a new psychology of learning, and a new conception of the social character of the school, the Progressive educator was in a position to interpret the educational significance and possibilities of the complete range of human behavior in all its biological, intellectual, and social aspects. From this point of view he could see that learning was an active and purposive doing, and that such doings, as educative, led on continuously from one activity to another, each growing progressively into larger and more satisfactory experiences. He was also in a position to see that the character of the educative activity was social in its most fundamental sense, that the school was an integral part of the community, and that education in its widest meaning and effect was carried on in the normal activities of everyday life.[3]

In the light of such basic conceptions the Progressive reaction to the traditional school was opposed to the older view that secondary education was merely a preparation for "future" life.

---

[3] A more systematic and detailed analysis of Progressive views is given in Chapter II.

Present needs and *present* living were emphasized. The "subject" curriculum was discredited, and in various ways the Progressive schools sought to develop a program which would enrich the present living of pupils, and would also lead on to their continuous development and satisfactory induction into the adult community.

The democratic implications of such a position are obvious. The respect for the individual, the attempt to develop an educational program based upon *his* peculiar interests and capacities, and the dominant conception of "needs": all of these clearly indicate that Progressive ideas have been strongly influenced by the democratic tradition.

However, the possible concrete meanings of Progressive education, with respect to the secondary school curriculum, are not yet wholly clear. The concept of "needs" and its ambiguous meaning in the Progressive movement was discussed at some length in a previous chapter. Here, it is sufficient to emphasize that the dominant tendencies in Progressive curriculum revision have consistently reflected the widest concern over a program suited to the "needs" of youth. In this regard, the development of the "core" curriculum has been discussed and particular questions were raised regarding the possible inadequacies of the type of program planned by adolescents and teachers in the local school with little or no regard for large-scale educational planning and leadership based on inclusive social vision—this in view of the assumption that the "core" curriculum tends to reflect the most fundamental and inclusive problems of American life, whether in their personal or in their social aspects.[4]

The tendency among some Progressive educators to regard the "subjects," as such, with distrust, and to urge continually for the more completely "psychological" organization of the curriculum, was also critically reviewed. It was suggested that education at the secondary level increasingly requires the organization of learnings on a systematic basis, and that effective participation in this complex and highly organized society demands a continuity and systematic development of experience

---

[4] This matter was discussed in Chapter IV, 103 ff.

which too often appears to be lacking in the Progressive school.

At this point, however, it should be noted that the lack of continuity of experience in secondary education cannot be attributed wholly to Progressive tendencies. It must be recognized that the Progressive school is often vastly superior in this respect to the traditional one in which the "subjects" are likely to be largely without meaning or pertinence to the activities of the pupil. Continuity of experience is not assured by "subjects," as such, nor by the expressed "interests" of pupils, aside from conditions which lead to the cumulative growth of such interests.

No doubt the very complexity of modern industrial society, and its ramifying functions, was in some degree a significant influence in the extension of the American common school to include a longer period of systematic preparation for participation in modern life. Unfortunately, in recent years the character of this demand appears to have been somewhat obscured by frustrating social conditions, on the one hand,· and the partially unconscious discouragement of educators who have tended to adapt the school program to the common (and not unwarranted) assumption that it is useless to attempt to educate a large proportion of American youth with respect to any definite occupational functions in society. Too often, the discrediting of the "college-preparatory" curriculum on the basis of the fact that a large proportion of youth do not go into the colleges is also taken to mean that young people are not going into any kind of special activity for which the public school might help to lay an intensive and significant preparation. One wonders if there may not be a measure of suggestive truth in the contention of some educators that the philosophy of "interest" and "pupil freedom" was used to "accommodate the mass education movement" in the American schools.[5] The criticism, however, would seem more nearly sound if it were to take account of the social and economic factors which attended the rise of the universal public high school.

If the "philosophy of interest" has been used to "rationalize"

[5] Specific reference is made to Bagley's criticism as cited in Chapter III, 72 ff.

anything in American education it would seem to be not so much the "lowering of scholastic standards" as the lowering of opportunities for the participation of American youth in activities which would give meaning to systematic and rigorous scholarship in the schools. The "activity" school has no meaning if its activities are sham. The Progressive high school will not be able to fulfill its contract as Progressive *or* as democratic until it is able to provide a curriculum based on social and educational conditions which will provide a suitable medium for the normal development and growth of the activities of youth in American life.

A Functional Curriculum for an Industrial Society

It is proposed, therefore, that a more suitable curriculum for American youth should be based on a rounded program of functional activities leading on gradually and continuously to adult status in the affairs of community life. This would mean, among other things, that significant occupational *experiences of some kind should be provided for all youth during the period of secondary education.* This statement needs some elaboration. It will require, in the first place, a psychological interpretation.

In the writings of Dewey there are a number of references to what he terms, in effect, an occupational pattern of behavior. This conception, in large outline, holds that within a "functional" view of mind man's habits, and the meanings and values which he associates with the objects of his environment, are determined by fundamental modes of activity, or occupations. The following quotation from Dewey is illustrative:

. . . The biological point of view commits us to the conviction that mind, whatever else it may be, is at least an organ of service for the control of environment in relation to the ends of the life process.

If we search in any social group for the special functions to which mind is thus relative, occupations at once suggest themselves. Occupations determine the fundamental modes of activity, and hence control the formation and use of habits. These habits, in turn, are something more than practical and overt. "Apperceptive masses" and associational tracts of necessity conform to the dominant activities. The occupations determine the chief modes of satisfaction,

the standards of success and failure. Hence they furnish the working classifications and definitions of value; they control the desire
processes. Moreover, they decide the sets of objects and relations
that are important, and thereby provide the content or material of
attention, and the qualities that are interestingly significant. The
directions given to mental life thereby extend to emotional and
intellectual characteristics. So fundamental and pervasive is the
group of occupational activities that it affords the scheme or pattern
of the structural organization of mental traits. Occupations inte-
grate special elements into a functioning whole.[6]

Human behavior is structured, that is, by the way in which
man seeks to control the environment in living, by the way in
which he *makes a living*. The latter term, of course, is not to
be limited to the ordinary meaning of "having a job for pay."
The term "function" is suggested here as having the somewhat
broader connotation of any prominent patterning function of
social life, such as "being a parent," "making a home," or "being
an engineer." It must be remembered, however, that the occupation, in its limited "vocational" sense, tends in modern industrial
society to order the other functions and habits of daily living. A
person is known primarily by what he "does." His intellectual
and emotional life is patterned, first of all, by the primary fact
that he is a doctor, an artist, or a mechanic, living and working,
of course, in this particular society. It is largely through one's
work, through his functional participation in the activities of
community life, that his intellectual dispositions and emotional
attitudes take form.

Thus to assume that secondary education can pretend to bring
young men and women to intellectual maturity and to understanding of American life aside from occupational experiences
leading to gradually increasing participation (wherever possible)
would appear dubious. It is to be noted, in this regard, that
many young people do "grow up" into competent and understanding adulthood, at least by present standards. It is also true,
of course, that the cultural exclusion of youth is never complete. Most boys and girls mature in a family environment and
take part in various community functions. Some gain employ-

[6] John Dewey, "Interpretation of the Savage Mind," in *Philosophy and Civilization*, pp. 175–176. Minton, Balch and Company, New York, 1931.

ment while in school. But one major fact remains: In the vast majority of cases, the American youth of high school age, and often beyond, remains a social infant so far as his maturing intellectual dispositions and allegiances in community life depend upon his occupational status in the present industrial society.

As a matter of fact, the contention that secondary education should be based upon the functional-occupational experiences of youth is not as revolutionary as it first might appear. All education is actually occupational or "vocational" in its primary sense. The liberal arts curriculum of the ancient and medieval periods was an occupational education for the young men of that time, as some educational historians have suggested. Rhetoric and logic, for instance, were at one time essential vocational tools to young men in public life whose success was in some large measure dependent upon their expressive powers of eloquence and persuasion. And for that matter, the less "practical" elements in the "liberal arts" program were also part of a definite training for the leisure-life of the privileged groups.

In American education, Dewey suggested some years ago that the elementary school was actually a *vocational* school but that it stood for a restricted type of clerical training which was charged with non-democratic implications.[7] As for the present American high school, the case is clear. As stated in a recent report of a committee sponsored by the American Council on Education, ". . . The secondary schools emphasize today, as they always have, preparation for occupations of the professional and clerical type—the so-called 'white-collar' jobs. . . ." Significantly, the report goes on to say that ". . . Any examination of the opportunities that are really open makes it clear that the hopes fostered by the present educational system are sure to be disappointed for most of those now registered in secondary schools."[8]

We are living in an industrial society, and as Dewey indicated

---

[7] See Chapter I, pp. 24 ff.

[8] *What the High Schools Ought to Teach*, p. 10. (The Report of a Special Committee on the Secondary School Curriculum. Prepared for the American Youth Commission and Other Cooperating Agencies.) American Council on Education, Washington, D. C., 1940.

some years ago, "The real issue is not the question whether an industrial education is to be added on to a more or less mythical cultural elementary education, but what sort of industrial education we are to have." [9] Dewey's statement, which was made in a discussion of "dual" control of vocational education in 1917, has gathered new importance with the intervening years, but the present issue is continuous with the problem which Dewey considered at that time. Legally the problem of "dual" control has been eliminated in most states, but the problem of dual education continues.[10]

If secondary education *is* occupational in character, and if it *is* committed to the democratic ideal of equality of educational opportunity, then it appears that significant and fruitful occupational experiences should be provided in a common school environment. Otherwise, a large proportion of American youth will continue to find the high school a false promise, and a temporary refuge from an "outside" world, while the vast majority of young men and women will continue to make their most crucial adjustments to modern living without benefit of organized public education.

It might be unwarranted, of course, to assume that every high school youth ought to have part-time, remunerative employment while yet in school. No such sweeping assumption need be made. But it seems clear that all American youth should have meaningful and frequent contacts with a wide variety of occupational activities, as representing the industrial community, at large, and that such contacts should lead through successive and gradual stages of observation, exploration, trial experiences, and functional participation in the activities, themselves.[11] The immediate object would be twofold: To give every youth a rounded and first-hand conception of the occupational life of the community, in its many phases, and to provide a basis

[9] Quoted in Chapter I, p. 24.

[10] See Chapter I, p. 25.

[11] A highly suggestive proposal, showing some of the concrete possibilities which might be developed in a high school program, such as that suggested by the writer, is given by Goodwin Watson, "A Program for American Youth," in *A Challenge to Secondary Education* (Samuel Everett, edr.) , Chap. VII, pp. 151–174. D. Appleton-Century Company, New York, 1935.

of deliberate occupational selection on the grounds of personal capacities and interests as brought out through trial experiences, on the one hand, and professional guidance, on the other. The more inclusive educative purpose would be to bring the crucial educational possibilities of the period of occupational adjustment within the control of a common educational environment. Only in this way can education most effectively help to infuse the industrial life of this society with the common meanings and values of American democracy. To repeat Dewey's injunction, the question is not whether we shall have industrial education, but what kind of industrial education we shall have.

The Occupational Orientation in Education

To avoid possible misunderstanding, some further notes should be made with regard to the meaning of the terms "occupation" and "occupational" in this study. Dewey's discussion of occupations as determining fundamental modes of activity and controlling habits has been cited. In this broad sense the occupation is considered the dominant factor in the structure of human behavior. It is the occupation which exercises the greatest and most pervasive influence in the life of the individual. It is through his occupational activities that the individual attains stature as a person, and meaning as a member of society. "Occupational" education, in this sense, might well be considered a redundant term since all education is presumably the effort to foster the development of the individual and to help him form and release his constructive powers in a social medium. An education which is not occupational, in this sense would be unthinkable from the standpoint of a functional view of mind.

Unfortunately, the term "occupation" sometimes appears to carry with it the Biblical curse of Adam who brought work upon mankind as the product of his sin. Perhaps the most obvious danger in the use of the term "occupational," as denoting a basic organizing principle for secondary education, is that it might suggest a merely "utilitarian" type of "bread-and-butter" training for vocation. This, of course, is precisely the type of education that most young men and women now receive, *after they leave the public schools.* The case for a high school program properly oriented to the important educational implications of the facts of occupational adjustment in the lives of young men and women would be detrimental last of all to the values so often represented as "general education."

One sometimes encounters the argument that technological progress is gradually releasing mankind from the exhaustive and deadening labor of production, that machines will be utilized to do more and more of the world's work, and that man's energies will be freed for the greater enjoyment of leisure-time pursuits and for greater participation in social and political activities of a "non-vocational" type. Unfortunately the measure of truth in this line of reasoning tends to be distorted by the tacit assumption that the occupational life of man is somehow sordid, and tainted with the spirit of gross material gain—that the educational foundations of a better social and political existence must be independently established first, and that planned occupational or vocational education should be reserved in large measure for some vague period above and beyond the time of youth education.

It should be noted, first, that while modern man is in a position technologically to reduce the deadening effects of mechanized and routinized labor, this state of affairs does not necessarily reduce his occupational existence. The educational significance of a man's occupational activity is not determined primarily by whether he is to work twelve hours a day, or four. Obviously, it is necessary and desirable to control the working hours and other conditions of labor, but in a functional society it would seem also to be desirable to establish conditions for the optimum release of the creative and productive energies of each individual. No doubt it is important to educate for "leisure," but it is highly questionable whether such education should be based on the simple assumption that "leisure" education becomes important in inverse ratio to the length of the work-day. It would seem rather that a sound program of "leisure" education should be based first of all upon an enriched conception of occupation, or work. It is a psychological platitude that leisure-time pursuits become genuinely satisfying and recreative when they are properly balanced by dominant and sustained activities of a productive type. But the relation of education for work and education for leisure is only one aspect of the problem.

More fundamental, perhaps, is the common misconception that secondary education can, and should, bring young men and women to social and political maturity largely prior to their systematic study of, and actual participation in, the occupational activities of the community life. To show that such a position is rationalistic, as well as psychologically unsound, is in part the purpose of the succeeding pages. But one other comment should be made at this point. The particular meaning of occupation is always a function of a particular culture. If occupational or vocational education is considered to be linked with non-educative, or miseducative influences of a work-a-day world, it is presumably the economic and political conditions of work which should be taken into account—not the fact of work, or education for work, itself. At the same time it is held that man's habits as a political and social being are patterned and controlled by his functional work activities. Hence, to assume that any full measure of political and social understanding or competence is likely to be obtained apart from the contemporaneous induction of the individual into the occupational life of the society seems totally unwarranted.

Education, "Work," and Scholarship

Further educational implications of the work-pattern of human behavior are brought out in the distinctive character of learning in secondary education, as illustrated in the difference between "work" and "play." In early childhood the development of experience is carried on in a world of "*play*." The typical childhood attitudes of extreme freedom and irresponsibility are suitable and necessary to the child's development so long as his primary function is to take on the elementary meanings, conventions, and attitudes of the group life. In the older child, the youth, and the young adult the pattern of development gradually changes through imperceptible stages to the attitude of *"work."* This attitude, as described by Dewey, is ". . . an interest in an activity as tending to a culmination . . . and therefore possessing a thread of continuity binding together its successive stages. . . ." [12] "Work," in other words, leads to consequences which make a difference in "real" life and therefore entails responsibility to something other than the mere "play" world of fancy and imagination which can be "switched on and off" at will.

Hence, the normal transition which occurs between childhood and adulthood is one which necessarily involves the *gradual and actual* induction of youth into responsible "work" activities which have continuity and significance in the "real" world. Any other conception must temporize either by attempting to hold the youth in an "academic" realm of "knowledge," as merely preparatory for living, or by attempting to base the curriculum on an extended child-world of "adolescent needs" [13] which offers complementary "activities" in compensation for the deficits of an "outside" and unreceptive world of "reality." Such activities are unsatisfactory for youth education and for significant personal growth because they are essentially abortive and disappointing. They lack the *continuity* of "work" as representing activities intrinsically worth while in the sense that they are sustained and carried progressively forward by their own results in an environment yielding increasingly satisfying returns.

The fundamental condition of personal growth and continuity of experience in secondary education is also the condition of a sound and intensive attitude of scholarship which would support the kind of systematic intellectual growth so often missing in the secondary school.

There is, of course, no conclusive statistical evidence to show that scholarship is missing in the secondary schools, unless one is prepared to accept the assumption that scholarship may be

[12] John Dewey, *How We Think*, p. 213. D. C. Heath and Company, New York, 1933. (New Edition.)

[13] As pointed out in Chapter II, this term is used with different meanings. It is used here to illustrate only *one*.

determined on the basis of an arbitrary standard of scholastic "achievement." If comparisons between American high school students and those of European secondary schools are to be made it is only too obvious that scholastic "achievement" must be measured with respect to some common standards which certainly should not be expressed in terms of mere "book knowledge." However, it is entirely probable that European secondary school students *do* have a more serious attitude toward their school experiences, as some critics of Progressive education have maintained. The Progressive answer to this criticism, namely, that the outcomes of American secondary education are to be measured not in terms of "subject matter" learned, but in terms of personal growth, however, is not wholly convincing. Once more the question is raised whether the rounded growth of the individual in a complex industrial society does not require the intensive and systematic intellectual development which can only be sustained by functional participation in an on-going activity which makes constantly enlarging demands in terms of new understandings and techniques.

The assumption that such development can take place without a good deal of systematic learning involving the sustained use of symbols and "book" materials was discussed in a preceding chapter.[14] It may be added here that the common attitude regarding the opposition of careful scholarship and occupational education, as suggested by the term "vocational," is a highly artificial conception belonging to the aristocratic classical and European tradition of secondary and higher education. The persistence of this tradition in the modern American school has been noted. The time is long overdue when secondary education should take account of Dewey's observation that the sciences actually grew out of the occupations:

The history of culture shows that mankind's scientific knowledge and technical abilities have developed, especially in all their earlier stages, out of the fundamental problems of life. Anatomy and physiology grew out of the practical needs of keeping healthy and active; geometry and mechanics out of demands for measuring land, for building, and for making labor-saving machines; astronomy has

[14] See Chapter III.

been closely connected with navigation, keeping record of the passage of time; botany grew out of the requirements of medicine and of agronomy; chemistry has been associated with dyeing, metallurgy, and other industrial pursuits. In turn, modern industry is almost wholly a matter of applied science; year by year the domain of routine and crude empiricism is narrowed by the translation of scientific discovery into industrial invention. The trolley, the telephone, the electric light, the steam engine, with all their revolutionary consequences for social intercourse and control, are the fruits of science.[15]

The broad implications of Dewey's statement should not be limited to the "natural" sciences, but may well apply to all of the informed activities of society as based on past experience and the findings of experimental scientific method. The point is simply that systematic studies and scholarship find their proper place in the high school curriculum when they are integrally related to the present and growing activities of youth according to the peculiar interests and capacities of each individual.

However, the meaning of intellectual growth as based on the occupational experiences of youth is broader than mere "scholarship" in the sense of the increasing capacity of the individual to carry out a given function. As already indicated, the primary purpose of the conceived program would be not merely to increase the powers of the individual but to provide a socio-educational environment in which the most inclusive conditions of personal growth would be taken into account. The possible meaning of the "core" curriculum with respect to this aspect of the problem may now be reconsidered.

The "Core" Curriculum

In the preceding chapter it was suggested that the "core" curriculum emerged as a special part of the school program in the presence of crucial changes in American society, that it is concerned with the broadly social aspects of human activities, and that it represents those personal-social problems which are common to the lives of American youth. In view of these observations, it was concluded that the development of a significant

[15] John Dewey, *How We Think*, p. 216. D. C. Heath and Company, New York, 1933. (New Edition.)

"core" program calls for common social and educational resources which are commensurate to the problems at hand.

The more concrete implications of this statement should now
be clear. If the writer's assumptions regarding the character of
the problem in secondary education are valid, it is apparent that
the "core" curriculum is at bottom the educational aspect of the
most inclusive problems in American life. If secondary education is to be based on the functional participation of youth in
modern industrial society it is only too obvious that this problem alone will require planning and effort on a nation-wide
scale.

It should be added at once that the utilization of the most inclusive social resources and leadership in youth education would
in no way need to conflict with the fundamental values of local
initiative and local planning in education. If "local initiative"
and the "autonomous" school unit are to keep their democratic
meaning it will be not because they are opposed to wide-scale
planning, but because they are supported by resources commensurate to the national aspects of problems which have long
since lost their local character in an integrating society. With
respect to the problem of central planning and leadership in
secondary education, a recent report sponsored by the American
Council on Education makes the following statement:

What this country needs today is clear insight into the youth
problem, willingness to marshal the most competent individuals to
work out a new program of induction of youth into adulthood,
prestige behind the findings of such a group of competent individuals, and a vigorous campaign that will make the plans for reform
known to the American public.
. . . While it is not contemplated that the federal government
exercise authority over the schools, leadership by the Office of Education is needed, and will be welcomed more cordially than in
earlier times, because of the urgency of the problem of redirecting
the activities of secondary schools.
Some central organizing agency seems . . . to be necessary to
bring the issues of curriculum revision more prominently to the
attention of the general public and of teachers. . . .[16]

[16] *What the High Schools Ought to Teach*, pp. 35–36. (The Report of a
Special Committee on the Secondary School Curriculum. Prepared for the
American Youth Commission and Other Cooperating Agencies.) American
Council on Education, Washington, D. C., 1940.

This is a highly suggestive proposal. Of course, it is difficult to see how any amount of central educational planning and leadership will materially improve the situation unless such planning is also integrally related to an inclusive social effort to modify the socio-economic conditions which now obstruct the democratic purpose of the secondary school.

So far as the "core" stands for a curriculum based on the expressed "needs" of pupils the conception of a functional-occupational pattern for the secondary school curriculum presents significant implications. It will be recalled that Hutchins opposes the true function of "general education," i.e., "intellectual training," to the "vocationalism" of modern education. It appears that the Progressive school leans to a different position, but the explicit meaning of the Progressive alternative, or alternatives, is not wholly clear. As a matter of fact, there are indications, as already suggested, that some Progressive educators subscribe to a view which amounts to the tacit recognition that the school must provide a special environment for youth as set off from the deficiencies of the "outside" world. The following quotation from *Reorganizing Secondary Education* illustrates the point:

It is the primary thesis of this book that the supreme mission of secondary education at this time is to help young people realize the significant possibilities implicit in their changing status—to help them find themselves anew in their personal, social, and economic relationships, and to develop a working philosophy of values which will give meaning, zest, and purpose to their living. This is in large part the responsibility of the school: *life outside provides too little opportunity for participation and affords too little direction toward establishing young people in a rightful place of their own.*[17]

The rather wide practice in Progressive schools is to rely upon a program of "general education" which, if not opposed to industrial and specific occupational experience, is at least quite far removed from its possible effects. Of course, some Progressive schools do make provisions for part-time work experiences for limited numbers of students. However, we have seen that

[17] V. T. Thayer, Caroline B. Zachry, and Ruth Kotinsky, *Reorganizing Secondary Education*, p. 6. (A report for the Commission on the Secondary School Curriculum of the Progressive Education Association.) D. Appleton-Century Company, New York, 1939. (Italics mine.)

the broad tendency in American secondary education, whether Progressive or otherwise, is to cling to the traditional separation of "general" and "vocational" education.

The problem, apparently, is whether or not a significant program of "general education," or "core," can be defined on the basis of a system of youth education which persistently divides its potentially most significant intellectual experiences from a context which would give them vital content and meaning. The case for a "core" curriculum based upon the expressed "needs" of youth would carry much greater weight if the school program were actually to embrace activities leading on continuously to gradually increasing participation and responsibility in the affairs of community life. As pointed out in an earlier part of this chapter, social and intellectual maturity are not the automatic results of biological development in a pleasant and literate environment, however surcharged with the discussion of current social problems and "purposive" activities, unless the activities are actually leading somewhere. If the broadest educative effects of a common school environment are to be carried into American life it will have to be through a system of youth education which actually comes into living contact with the occupational functions that pattern the thinking and feeling of the maturing person.

The "Choice" of Youth Education

Finally, it may be noted that present social and educational resources for the gradual induction of youth into responsible participation in the functional life of society are wholly inadequate. Youth unemployment (aside from the special conditions of war), the youth work agencies, and the present status of vocational education provide the main evidence.[18] Taking into account special cases involving the cooperation of local industry or business as offering part-time work for students, it is only too apparent that the schools, as at present constituted, would find it highly difficult, and probably impossible, to meet the demand

[18] See Chapter I, pp. 25 ff.

for significant and functional work experiences of some kind for all pupils.

The objection might be raised at this point that the proposal of this study is visionary on the grounds of its own evidence. The answer is that the proposal is found in the implications of the American democratic tradition of the unitary public school and in the only constantly meaningful and fruitful conception of an activity curriculum providing the conditions of personal growth in this democratic-industrial society, from the writer's point of view. It would appear that a universal program of functional-occupational education for American youth entails some reconstruction of its social conditions, along with its own program. The problem of the schools is also the problem of American life. One of two courses is open: to reconsider the avowed aim of the American high school, as distinguished from its European antecedents, or to reconsider the conditions which now defeat such an aim. Thus, the "logical" argument is for a consistently honest and unequivocal approach to the problem of secondary education. If the argument is also "visionary" it is because it is based on the profound belief that American society and education will continue to move in the direction of their common democratic tradition.

BIBLIOGRAPHY

AIKEN, WILFORD M. "The Commission on the Relation of School and College." In *Educational Research Bulletin,* Vol. 17, No. 8. Ohio State University, Columbus, Ohio, 1938.

ALABAMA STATE DEPARTMENT OF EDUCATION. *Curriculum Bulletin No. 7, Planning the Core Curriculum in the Secondary School, Alabama Curriculum Development Program.* State of Alabama Department of Education, Department Bulletin 1940, No. 2. State Board of Education, Montgomery, Alabama, 1939.

AMERICAN COUNCIL ON EDUCATION. General Report of the American Youth Commission. *Youth and the Future.* American Council on Education, Washington, D. C., 1942.

AMERICAN COUNCIL ON EDUCATION. The Report of a Special Committee on the Secondary School Curriculum. *What the High Schools Ought to Teach.* Prepared for the American Youth Commission and Other Co-operating Agencies, American Council on Education, Washington, D. C., 1940.

BAGLEY, WILLIAM C. *Education and Emergent Man.* Thomas Nelson and Sons, New York, 1934.

BAGLEY, WILLIAM C. *Education, Crime, and Social Progress.* The Macmillan Company, New York, 1932.

BAGLEY, WILLIAM C. *The Educative Process.* The Macmillan Company, New York, 1922.

BAGLEY, WILLIAM C. "An Essentialist's Platform for the Advancement of American Education." In *Educational Administration and Supervision,* Vol. 24, April, 1938.

BAGLEY, WILLIAM C. "Is Subject Matter Obsolete?" In *Educational Administration and Supervision,* Vol. 21, No. 6, September, 1935.

BERNAL, J. D. *The Social Function of Science.* The Macmillan Company, New York, 1939.

BODE, BOYD H. *Progressive Education at the Crossroads.* Newson and Company, New York, 1938.

BRIGGS, THOMAS H. *Secondary Education.* The Macmillan Company, New York, 1937.

BRIGGS, THOMAS H. "A Vision of Secondary Education." In *Teachers College Record,* Vol. 34, October, 1932.

CALIFORNIA STATE DEPARTMENT OF EDUCATION. Bulletin, *Programs of the Co-operating Schools in California.* California State Department of Education, Sacramento, May, 1939.

CHILDS, JOHN L. *Education and the Philosophy of Experimentalism.* D. Appleton-Century Company, New York, 1931.

COOK, LLOYD ALLEN. *Community Backgrounds of Education.* McGraw-Hill Company, New York, 1938.

COUNTS, GEORGE S. "Current Practices in Curriculum-Making in Public High Schools." In *National Society for the Study of Education,* Vol. 26, Part I, Chap. 7, pp. 135–162. Public School Publishing Company, Bloomington, Illinois, 1926.

COUNTS, GEORGE S. *Dare the School Build a New Social Order?* John Day Company, New York, 1932.

COUNTS, GEORGE S. *Secondary Education and Industrialism.* Harvard University Press, Cambridge, 1929.

CURTI, MERLE. *The Social Ideas of American Educators.* Report of the Commission on the Social Studies, Pt. X. Charles Scribner's Sons, New York, 1935.

DAVIS, CALVIN OLIN. *Our Evolving High School Curriculum.* World Book Company, New York, 1927.

DEWEY, JOHN. *Democracy and Education.* The Macmillan Company, New York, 1916.

DEWEY, JOHN. *Experience and Education.* The Macmillan Company, New York, 1933.

DEWEY, JOHN. "The Higher Learning in America." In *The Social Frontier,* Vol. 3, No. 24, March, 1937.

DEWEY, JOHN. *How We Think.* D. C. Heath and Company, New York, 1933. (New Edition.)

DEWEY, JOHN. *Human Nature and Conduct.* The Modern Library, New York, 1922.

DEWEY, JOHN. "Interpretation of the Savage Mind." In *Philosophy and Civilization.* Minton, Balch and Company, New York, 1931.

DEWEY, JOHN. "Learning to Earn: The Place of Vocational Education in a Comprehensive Scheme of Public Education." In *School and Society,* Vol. 5, No. 117, March 24, 1917.

DEWEY, JOHN. *The School and Society.* The University of Chicago Press, Chicago, 1900.

DEWEY, JOHN. "Splitting Up the School System." In *New Republic,* Vol. 2, No. 24, April 17, 1915.

DEWEY, JOHN. "The Higher Learning in America." In *Social Frontier,* Vol. 3, No. 24, March, 1937.

DEWEY, JOHN. "President Hutchins' Proposals to Remake Higher Education." In *Social Frontier,* Vol. 3, No. 22, January, 1937.

DEWEY, JOHN. "Rationality in Education." In *Social Frontier,* Vol. 3, No. 21, December, 1936.

EBY, FREDERICK and ARROWOOD, CHARLES FLINN. *The Development of Modern Education.* Prentice-Hall, Inc., New York, 1934.

ESPY, HERBERT G. *The Public Secondary School; A Critical Analysis of Secondary Education in the United States.* Houghton Mifflin Company, Boston, 1939.

EVERETT, SAMUEL. *A Challenge to Secondary Education.* Society for Curriculum Study, Committee on Secondary Education. D. Appleton-Century Company, New York, 1935.

EVERETT, SAMUEL. (Edr.) *The Changing Curriculum.* D. Appleton-Century Company, New York, 1935.

GILES, H. H., McCUTCHEON, S. P., and ZECHIEL, A. N. *Exploring the Curriculum, Adventure in American Education,* Vol. 2. Commission on the Relation of School and College of the Progressive Education Association. Harper and Brothers, New York, 1942.

GOULD, LESLIE A. *American Youth Today.* Random House, New York, 1940.

HAYES, CARLTON J. H. *A Political and Cultural History of Modern Europe,* Vol. I. The Macmillan Company, New York, 1933.

HOGBEN, LANCELOT. *The Retreat from Reason.* Watts and Company, London, 1936.

HOPKINS, L. THOMAS. *Integration: Its Meaning and Application.* D. Appleton-Century Company, New York, 1937.

HUTCHINS, ROBERT MAYNARD. *The Higher Learning in America.* Yale University Press, New Haven, 1936.

HUTCHINS, ROBERT MAYNARD. "Ideals in Education." In *The American Journal of Sociology,* Vol. 43, No. 1, July, 1937.

HUTCHINS, ROBERT MAYNARD. "The Philosophy of Education." In *The William Rainey Harper Memorial Conference.* (Robert N. Montgomery, edr.) The University of Chicago Press, Chicago, 1937.

HUTCHINS, ROBERT MAYNARD. "A Reply to Professor Whitehead." In *Atlantic Monthly,* Vol. 158, November, 1936.

JUDD, CHARLES H. *Education and Social Progress.* Harcourt, Brace and Company, New York, 1934.

JUSTMAN, JOSEPH. *Theories of Secondary Education in the United States.* Bureau of Publications, Teachers College, Columbia University, New York, 1940.

KANDEL, I. L. *History of Secondary Education.* Houghton Mifflin Company, Boston, 1930.

KILPATRICK, WILLIAM H. Edr. *The Educational Frontier.* D. Appleton-Century Company, New York, 1933.

KILPATRICK, WILLIAM H. *The Project Method; The Use of the Purposeful Act in the Educative Process.* Bureau of Publications, Teachers College,

Columbia University, New York, 1921. (Reprint from *Teachers College Record,* September, 1918.)

KILPATRICK, WILLIAM H. *Remaking the Curriculum.* Newson and Company, New York, 1936.

MANNHEIM, KARL. *Ideology and Utopia.* Harcourt, Brace and Company, New York, 1935.

MISSISSIPPI STATE DEPARTMENT OF EDUCATION. *Bulletin No. 7, Mississippi Program for the Improvement of Instruction, Curriculum Reorganization in the Secondary School, Grades 7–12.* State Department of Education, Jackson, Mississippi, October, 1939.

MORRISON, HENRY C. *The Curriculum and the Common School.* The University of Chicago Press, Chicago, 1940.

NATIONAL EDUCATION ASSOCIATION. *Report of the Committee of Ten on Secondary School Studies.* American Book Company, New York, 1894.

NATIONAL EDUCATION ASSOCIATION. *Report of the Committee on College Entrance Requirements.* University of Chicago Press, Chicago, 1899.

NATIONAL EDUCATION ASSOCIATION, EDUCATIONAL POLICIES COMMISSION. *The Civilian Conservation Corps, The National Youth Administration, and the Public Schools.* National Education Association of the United States and the American Association of School Administrators, Washington, D. C., 1941.

NATIONAL EDUCATION ASSOCIATION, EDUCATIONAL POLICIES COMMISSION. *The Unique Function of Education in American Democracy.* National Education Association of the United States and the Department of Superintendence, Washington, D. C., 1937.

NATIONAL EDUCATION ASSOCIATION, RESEARCH DIVISION. *Research Bulletin, Vol. 7, No. 4, Vitalizing the High School Curriculum.* Research Division of the National Education Association, Washington, D. C., 1929.

PLATO. *The Republic.* (Translation by B. Jowett.) The Dial Press, New York.

PROGRESSIVE EDUCATION ASSOCIATION. *Progressive Education Advances.* D. Appleton-Century Company, New York, 1938.

RAINEY, HOMER P. *How Fare American Youth?* D. Appleton-Century Company, New York, 1938.

RAINEY, HOMER P. "Social Factors Affecting General Education." In *Thirty-Eighth Yearbook of the National Society for the Study of Education,* Pt. II, *General Education in the American College.* (Guy Montrose Whipple, edr.) Public School Publishing Company, Bloomington, Illinois, 1939.

REISNER, EDWARD H. *The Evolution of the Common School.* The Macmillan Company, New York, 1930.

RUGG, HAROLD. *Democracy and the Curriculum.* D. Appleton-Century Company, New York, 1939.

RUSSELL, JOHN DALE and ASSOCIATES. *Vocational Education.* Prepared for the Advisory Committee on Education. United States Government Printing Office, Washington, D. C., 1938.

SPEARS, HAROLD. *The Emerging High School Curriculum.* American Book Company, New York, 1940.

STOUT, JOHN ELBERT. *The Development of High-School Curricula in the North Central States from 1860 to 1918.* The University of Chicago Press, Chicago, 1921.

THAYER, V. T., ZACHRY, CAROLINE, and KOTINSKY, RUTH. *Reorganizing Secondary Education.* Report of the Commission on Secondary Curriculum of the Progressive Education Association. D. Appleton-Century Company, New York, 1939.

THORNDIKE, EDWARD L. and SYMONDS, PERCIVAL M. "Occupations of High School Graduates and Non-Graduates." In *School Review,* Vol. 30, January, 1922.

UNITED STATES DEPARTMENT OF COMMERCE, BUREAU OF THE CENSUS. *Statistical Abstract of the United States, 1940.* Government Printing Office, Washington, D. C.

UNITED STATES OFFICE OF EDUCATION. *Biennial Survey of Education,* Bulletin 1937, No. 2. Government Printing Office, Washington, D. C., 1939.

UNITED STATES OFFICE OF EDUCATION, FEDERAL SECURITY AGENCY. *Statistics of Public High Schools, 1937–1938.* Bulletin 1940, No. 2, Chap. V. Government Printing Office, Washington, D. C., 1940.

UNITED STATES OFFICE OF EDUCATION, DEPARTMENT OF THE INTERIOR. *Offerings and Registrations in High School Subjects.* Bulletin 1938, No. 6. Government Printing Office, Washington, D. C., 1938.

VIRGINIA STATE BOARD OF EDUCATION. *Tentative Course of Study for the Core Curriculum of Secondary Schools.* Bulletin, Vol. 17, No. 2. Virginia State Board of Education, Richmond, Virginia, August, 1934.

VIRGINIA STATE BOARD OF EDUCATION. *Brief Description of the Virginia Program for Improving Instruction.* Bulletin, Vol. 21, No. 4. Virginia State Board of Education, Richmond, Virginia, 1939.

VIRGINIA STATE BOARD OF EDUCATION. *Public Schools in Virginia.* Bulletin, Vol. 22, No. 4. Virginia State Board of Education, Richmond, Virginia, January, 1940.

WRIGHTSTONE, WAYNE J. *Appraisal of Experimental High School Practices.* Bureau of Publications, Teachers College, Columbia University, New York, 1936.